Life
Is What Happens
When
You're Making Other Plans

Previous Books by the Author:

I SHOULD HAVE SEEN IT COMING WHEN THE RABBIT
DIED
UP A FAMILY TREE
MURPHY MUST HAVE BEEN A MOTHER!
(AND OTHER LAWS I LIVE BY)

TERESA BLOOMINGDALE

Life
Is What Happens
When
You're Making Other Plans

Doubleday & Company, Inc.
Garden City, New York
1984

Library of Congress Cataloging in Publication Data

Bloomingdale, Teresa, date
Life Is What Happens When You're Making Other Plans

1. Family—Nebraska—Anecdotes, facetiae, satire, etc.
2. Children—Nebraska—Anecdotes, facetiae, satire, etc.
3. Women authors—Nebraska—Anecdotes, facetiae, satire, etc.
4. Women authors—Nebraska—Biography.
5. Bloomingdale, Teresa, date. I. Title
HQ555.N2B549 1984   306.8'092'4   83–45344
ISBN: 0-385-18064-0

This book is dedicated, with much love,
to my children
Lee, John, Michael, Jim,
Mary, Dan, Peggy,
Ann, Tim, and
Patrick
The fortunate results of my making other plans!

Contents

Acknowledgment

My sincere thanks to my mother,
Helen Cooney Burrowes,
and my sister,
Madeleine Burrowes Sanders,
for their inspiration and assistance
in writing the verses for this book.

Introduction

I've made so many plans that have been changed
By circumstances out of my control
That I've resigned myself and since arranged
To let those "circumstances" be my goal.

INTRODUCTION

I am often asked why I, a busy mother of ten children, suddenly decided, on the brink of middle age, to seek an even busier career as newspaper columnist, book critic, magazine writer, lecturer on the national circuit, author, and frequent guest on radio and television talk shows.

Who sought it? Certainly not I. I was much too involved with birthday parties, car pools, dental appointments, homework schedules, house rules, and appropriate punishments to think about a career, for heaven's sakes. I already had a more-than-full-time career, thank you, and while I admit I loved it, I also admit that I was eagerly looking forward to retiring to my rocking chair where I would do nothing more exciting than sing lullabies to my grandbabies.

Which probably explains why, one week when I was particularly busy planning one son's graduation and another son's wedding, I suddenly found myself on "Hour Magazine" happily chatting with host Gary Collins about my newest book, my busy lecture schedule, and my hilarious experiences on other television shows.

The old adage is true: Life is what happens when you're making other plans, and no one should know this better than

I. For as far back as I can remember, my life has been playing havoc with my plans.

When I was in high school, I spent four years planning on going to an expensive and exclusive college in San Francisco. My heart went to San Francisco, but the rest of me went to Omaha. I had studied so hard to pass the rigid entrance exams for the California college, I won a scholarship to its sister school in Omaha. (I offered to forgo the scholarship and spend my parents' money, but I got outvoted.)

My college education was meant to lead to a career in television journalism, but like many women of that era, I happily discarded my career in favor of marriage (though God knows how I ever reached the altar, so well planned was our wedding).

I intended to work for a while before we started our family, but God beat us to the start. My first post-honeymoon paycheck was set aside for maternity clothes.

In the next twelve years my husband and I had ten children, none of whom were planned, though I'm sure they would have been had we had time to do so.

From the beginning I was hooked on motherhood, and I planned to spend the rest of my life just rocking babies, chasing toddlers, arguing with teenagers, accepting collect calls from college kids, planning weddings, and rocking more babies.

But someplace between the baby's bath and *his* baby's bath I got conned into writing a newspaper column, a humorous chronicle of family life, and later book reviews.

Perhaps, subconsciously, I once planned to become a columnist, as my father was before me, but I never planned to write a book. Writing a column can be fun, but writing a book is hard work! I should know; I've written four of them.

One aspect of my career that was not only not *planned,* but was definitely and emphatically planned *not,* was lecturing. I knew that many writers and authors lectured, but not this one! Nobody was going to drag *me* up onto a podium to make a fool of myself before an audience!

So of course I now go all over the country giving speeches, delighting in the laughter of my audience, and loving every minute of it. Thank heavens I made other plans!

The only plans I ever made that actually evolved were those concerning television, but even those were rescheduled by my life. For while I have finally fulfilled my college plans to appear on television, I have never been an anchorperson or a talk show host; I am always the guest, a role that is a lot more fun.

As my previous books, *I Should Have Seen It Coming When the Rabbit Died, Up a Family Tree,* and *Murphy Must Have Been a Mother,* were about the humorous aspects of my life as a mother, this book is about the funny things that have happened to me in my other life, as author, writer, lecturer, talk show guest, etc.

For many readers the best chapters will be those on "etc." For while some of you have, in the past, related to my experiences as a mother, and many of you will, now, relate to my experiences as a career woman, *all* of you have experienced the episodes in "etc."

Have fun!

The Author

Life
Is What Happens
When
You're Making Other Plans

A Comedy of Manners

Manners and morals, alas, are passé,
They're as dead as my Christmas poinsettia.
Virtue is rare, and "living-in" 's fair,
But of course these things mustn't fret ya.

Gone is the day when a lady's array
On feminine beauty was centered.
She never had heard of a four-letter word
And gentlemen rose when she entered.

Now jeans are the rule and sneakers are cool
And shoulders are bared to the sunning.
A tag must adhere to the right of the rear,
Otherwise you are out of the running.

But perhaps when the pendulum swings,
And custom again retrogresses,
Then couples will wed before they're abed,
And we'll know which are girls by their dresses.

1

A COMEDY OF MANNERS

Women who wait until middle age to launch a career often learn, to their dismay, that all the wisdom, knowledge, self-confidence, and sophistication they acquired as wives and mothers will not necessarily help them through certain sticky situations in which they may find themselves once they go out-in-the-world.

For example, I have hosted dozens of dinner parties during my at-home career as a wife and mother, and I have encountered just about every crisis imaginable, from the underdone entree to the overdone guest, from no towels in the bathroom to no guests at the party because I gave the wrong date. But nothing prepared me for the crisis I encountered the first time I hosted a dinner party as an author.

I was in Chicago, in the midst of a book promotion tour, so my husband was not with me when I decided to host a dinner party for some Chicago VIPs who had been most gracious to me during my stay in the Windy City. Because I really wanted to impress my guests, I took them to La Française, that famous five-star restaurant just outside Chicago, in Wheeling, Illinois.

As I expected, the dinner was magnificent. The food was delicious, the service superb, the ambience elegant. Everything was perfect, until time came to pay the check. As prearranged, the waiter slipped me the check, I slipped him my credit card, and he went off to pay the bill. In a few moments he returned to the table, bowed low over my chair, and whispered:

"I'm sorry, madam, but your credit card has been rejected."

I knew immediately what had happened. After twenty-some years of signing on my husband's credit card, I had, as I felt befitted my career, gotten my own credit card. But alas, I had forgotten about "new member limits" and in the past few days had blithely charged air fare, hotels, meals, and a rather indulgent afternoon of shopping at the Watertower. Before I ever walked into La Française the credit card company had shut me off.

A quick search of my purse confirmed the fact that I had no checkbook, just enough cash for taxi and tips, and only fifty dollars in traveler's checks. One does not host a dinner party at La Française for fifty dollars, unless perhaps *one* is the entire party. What to do?

In my "other" career, as a wife, I would have known exactly what to do. As my husband would have been co-hosting the dinner, it would have been *his* credit card that bounced, and my obligations would have been only twofold: (1) distract the guests while my husband handled the situation, and (2) never, ever mention the matter again.

Of course, had my husband been the host there would have been no such crisis because he would have been carrying a second major credit card as well as a veritable treasury in traveler's checks. And in the unlikely event that he misplaced those, there still would have been no problem, because the manager, acknowledging the executive aura that most men exude (at least those who eat at La Française!) would undoubtedly have said: "Don't trouble yourself, monsieur; we will be happy to bill you later."

But I had neither money nor aura, so I had no choice but to fall back on a talent I acquired years ago in yet another career, as a mother: humility. I turned to the guest I knew best and very humbly said: "I seem to be in a bit of a jam; would you perchance have a credit card I could borrow?" Fortunately, she did.

Since then I have encountered many "sticky situations" in my career as an author and lecturer, some indigenous to my own career, others which could happen to any woman, be she in business, a profession, the arts, or "just a housewife." I have found that the etiquette books cover many of these comedies of manners but not all.

Recently I received an invitation to a prenuptial party given in honor of some friends of ours who were getting married—she for the third time, he for the fourth. (I don't know where they find the energy!) I had heard that the prenuptial bash was to simulate the old-fashioned stag party, though the "modernist" host was including wives and girl friends. He was not, however, planning to exclude the traditional stag party entertainment. He had, in fact, indicated that while there would be no stag film, they "just might turn on the TV to the dirty movie channel; all for fun, of course."

Since no etiquette book I know of tells how a lady should react in such a situation, I called the etiquette expert, Letitia Baldrige, and put the problem to her. Tish replied that I needn't worry; no one turns on the television when they have guests! I said, "But what if they do?" and she suggested that I simply claim a headache and go home.

Rather than pester Tish with more "But what if's," I decided to write my own comedy of manners, which will include the following:

1. If you are hosting a restaurant party and suddenly find yourself without funds, you can
   a. pretend that you have prearranged payment and try to slip the entire party out of the restaurant unseen; if that doesn't work,
   b. turn to the most absentminded member of your party and say, "What a lovely party; thank you for inviting me!" And if that doesn't work,
   c. fall over on the table and play dead.

The only other alternative is to get arrested for stealing-a-meal, and I must say, if you are going to steal, I can't think of anything more worthwhile than a gourmet dinner at La Française.

2. You are the guest of honor at a large affair and some clod comes up to you and says, "I'll bet you don't remember me, do you?" You might say either
   a. "No, but we could have met before; you have a very forgettable face." Or
   b. "Of course I remember you! When did you get out of jail?" Or
   c. "I think so; didn't we meet at the White House reception for Prince Philip?" (The fact that you have never been to the White House is irrelevant.)

Personally I prefer that last reply, as it can provoke two responses, either of which can be useful. The clod will be intimidated by your importance and will therefore make a hasty retreat, or he actually may have been at the White House reception for Prince Philip, in which case he may be a clod worth cultivating.

3. Your job, or career, is such that your name appears frequently in the news media, in press releases, on posters, signs, etc., and unfortunately it is often misspelled. You can either

   a. spend half your life complaining (to the press, committee chairpersons, agencies, etc.) to little avail;

   b. change your name to the most frequently misspelled version (I am still trying to choose between Theresa and Tricia);

   c. ignore it. (You might as well, for it will happen again and again, especially if you have a name as difficult as my friend's, Mary Awsiukiewicz. People keep spelling it "Mari.")

4. You walk into a cocktail party and find that your boss's wife is wearing a six-hundred-dollar designer original, and you are wearing the sixty-dollar off-the-rack copy:

   a. Lock yourself in the bathroom until the boss and his wife go home (choose a downstairs bathroom, just in case they *are* home);

   b. light a cigarette, drop the match, and set fire to the place;

   c. plan an early retirement (from your job, not your evening). (Actually this is not a very serious situation; the sticky situation is going to occur when you try to convince your accountant, or your husband, or your daughter who wanted a new dress and you said you couldn't afford it, that you did not pay six hundred dollars for that dress.)

5. You are seated at the speaker's table at a very important banquet and you suddenly see an insect in your salad. You can either

   a. wait for the fellow on your right to turn to the person on *his* right, and quickly switch salads;

b. excuse yourself, leave the table, and go home, because if there's a bug in the salad, God only knows what's going to show up in the entree;

c. stand up and shout: "THERE'S A BUG IN MY SALAD!" (Haven't you ever wanted to do that? I have —even when there was no bug in my salad.)

6. You have recently lost your job, or you are currently not pursuing a career, and someone asks: "What do you do?" Suggested responses are

a. "Oh, nothing; I'm just a housewife!" (though of course they'll think you're bragging; who can afford to be "just a housewife" these days?);

b. "I'm a statistologist for the Department of Labor, currently doing research for the Equal Opportunity Commission" (nobody in their right mind would pursue that topic, unless it's another woman looking for a job and convinced she's being discriminated against because of her sex);

c. or you can give the response that's a favorite of my young adult offspring: "As little as possible."

7. You are being interviewed on television, or for the press, or simply to satisfy the curiosity of your questioner, and you are asked: "How old are you?"

a. If you are still under forty, go ahead and tell them exactly how old you are. Whatever your age, over half the country will envy you.

b. If you are over forty, add ten years to your age; it's so great to hear everybody whisper: "Gee, doesn't she look wonderful?"

c. If you are thirty-nine, lie. Nobody ever believes that anybody is thirty-nine.

8. You are filling out a job application, and you are offended by the question: "Please check your race: ( ) Caucasian ( ) Black ( ) Indian ( ) Asian."

I know of no better response than the one given by my friend Martin Luther King Hasakawa, who, when filling out his college application form, skipped over all those parenthetical choices and penciled in: "None of the above."

I do want to thank Tish Baldrige for advising me on what to do should I ever be subjected to watching those embarrassing porno films on TV. Sure enough, that prenuptial party host did turn on the "dirty movie" channel, but I didn't have to fake a headache and go home because before I got offended I got bored and fell asleep.

Such is the sophistication of middle age.

Least Favorite Things

Why do I let myself be thrown
By all life's irritations?
Do I indeed, if truth be known,
Anticipate vexations?

Is it a sign of middle age
That little things annoy me?
That survey sales arouse my rage
And barking dogs destroy me?

"Just make a list," the experts say,
"Of all you find upsetting."
They promise stress will melt away;
But one thing they're forgetting:

A PART OF ME RESISTS MAKING LISTS.

2

A FEW OF MY LEAST
FAVORITE THINGS

According to a magazine article I read recently, a quick cure for that all-American ailment, Depression-Anxiety-Hypertension (and if you don't have two out of three, you are either under the age of eight or you're an alien from outer space), is simply to make a list of all the things you "just can't stand," followed by the reasons why. The cure is supposed to come when you read over the list and realize how silly it is to waste your time and energy on such inane animosities, or perhaps when you read over the list and realize how discerning you are to hate so wisely and so well.

Unfortunately, most people will not avail themselves of this cure because they either (a) won't take the time to list all the things they hate, or (b) can't remember all the things they hate, or (c) refused to read the article because they have the rather ridiculous notion that they don't suffer from depression, anxiety, or hypertension.

Since I am periodically afflicted with one or another part of the above three-headed monster (depending on how many of my children are currently courting, being courted, awaiting results of final exams, or "temporarily" out of work), I immediately sat down and compiled a brief list of Things I Hate—and Why. Actually, the list could have been longer, but I had to cut it short because my husband needed the pencil. (Any of you who have school-age children will understand why we have only one pencil; some may be astounded that we have even one.)

So here are a few of my least favorite things:

1. VIDEO GAMES. My family and friends tell me that I hate video games because when I play them, I always lose, but that's not true. If I put my mind to it, and spent half as much time practicing as they do, I could bleep them all right off the tube. That, in fact, is what I hate about the video games: the noise. All those "bleep-bleep-bleep"'s, "chirp-chirp-chirp"'s and "duda-duda-DOO-duda-duda-DOO"'s drive me up the wall. It seems incredible to me that something so sophisticated and supposedly omniscient as a computer could be persuaded to utter such sophomoric sounds. I tried to convince my children that the video games would be much more challenging if they turned down the volume and played without sound, but they said it's not the same, and of course it isn't. Silent video games aren't nearly as much fun because they don't drive you out of your seat or up the wall.

2. RERUNS OF *CASABLANCA.* I realize that this admission may set me up for a Senate investigation on un-American activities, but surely I am not the only viewer who cannot bear to spend one more evening in Rick's Café Américaine. I have nothing against the movie itself; it was a great movie with a wonderful cast, and I admit that I still get teary when the "Marseillaise" drowns out "Die Wacht am Rhein." But my appreciation of *Casablanca* was spoiled years ago when I read a movie magazine "scoop" revealing one of the "secrets" involved in the making of the movie, a "secret" Bergman herself still smiled about years later but always refused to discuss. The "secret scoop"? It seems that Bogie was so much shorter than

Ingrid he had to stand on a box to kiss her. Now every time I watch those sentimental love scenes in *Casablanca,* I get the giggles at the image of Bogie-on-a-box. (I'm sorry, kids, but that's the way it was.)

3. COUPONS. I am not referring here to the coupons rich people clip off their tax-free bonds; I am talking about the coupons the rest of us are expected to cut out and keep track of until we go to the supermarket, where we can then get five cents off a jar of peanut butter (the giant size only), or a dime off a brand of detergent we have never heard of (and for good reason), or maybe even twenty cents off our favorite product (providing we buy it by the case).

We have all read articles about those people who claim they "cut $100 off our grocery bill by using coupons," but you'll notice the article never states whether that "cut" is for a month, a year, a decade, or a lifetime's worth of groceries. Nor do they ever mention how much time and energy coupon users spend (a) scanning the newspaper ads, (b) searching for a scissors, (c) clipping-on-the-dotted-line, (d) trying to find a place to file the coupons until you are ready to use them, (e) looking for them later because you forgot where you filed them, (f) finally taking them to the supermarket only to discover that they expired yesterday, or aren't valid in your state, or are for products that just got recalled.

I think discount coupons are not only a nuisance but a domestic hazard as well. Surely mine isn't the only husband who nags: "You mean you didn't use that coupon after I went to all the trouble to clip it for you? You could have gotten seven cents off a bushel of broccoli!" Since I don't want to put my marriage in jeopardy, I enthusiastically accept all the coupons my husband clips for me, but I never use them, even though I may be the only woman in America who buys peanut butter by the gallon and everything else by the case.

4. CLASS REUNIONS. Most people hate class reunions because they can't bear to have their former classmates see how much they have aged, but not me. I avoid class reunions because I don't like to dismay my aging classmates by letting them see how much younger I look than they do. It truly is remarkable, but I have not put on a pound, developed a wrinkle, or grown a gray hair since the day I graduated from college. For those of you who may be interested in my beauty formula, it is fantastically simple: Never step on a scale, never look in a mirror, and never, ever ask anybody "How do I look?" except your father.

5. WINDOWED ENVELOPES. I considered listing "junk mail," but then I remembered that some junk mail I actually enjoy, like Christmas catalogs. But I cannot ever remember receiving a windowed envelope that I welcomed, for windowed envelopes bear only bad news: bills, bank overdrafts, tax statements, begging letters, insurance premium notices. Let's face it; nobody ever got a love letter in a windowed envelope. Even worse are those windowed envelopes enclosed "for return payment." These particular windowed envelopes are most frustrating because the windows are invariably on the wrong side of the envelope. They must be; why else would I consistently note, after I have dutifully inserted my check and the return portion of the bill, and carefully sealed the envelope, that the window reveals only the back of the bill?

6. ELECTRONICALLY TYPED "PERSONALIZED" LETTERS. Even when they don't come in windowed envelopes I hate letters in which my name (usually misspelled) is interspersed throughout the message, thus trying to convince

me that said message was meant for me alone. I consider this an insult to my intelligence and am automatically "turned off" to the product or service, no matter how enticing it may be. I also resent the fact that the price for said product is hidden away in paragraph thirty-two, forcing me to read the entire letter before I conclude that I cannot afford to buy the darn thing even if I wanted to, which, by the time I have read through the letter, I almost always do.

7. PHONE CALLERS WHO LAUNCH THE CON-VERSATION WITH: "HI THERE! HOW ARE YOU TO-DAY?" I am always tempted to answer: "I am grouchy, grumpy, and broke, so don't try to sell me any house siding, carpet cleaning, or furnace overhauling." I do sympathize with anyone who is trying to earn a living selling something by telephone, but I resent the inquiry about my well-being (or lack thereof), as well as the long-winded, convoluted sales pitch. It seems to me they'd sell a lot more of their product if they'd launch the conversation with "Sorry to bother you, but I'm trying to earn a living; I don't suppose you want your house sided?"

8. BACKGROUND NOISE. I am not referring here to nature's "noises"—leaves rustling, birds singing, waves lapping the shore. Nor am I referring to necessary noise, such as that caused by traffic, trains, dishwashers, and garbage disposals (grating as they may be!). I am talking about that "noise" purposely imposed upon me by people who evidently think I cannot cope with a moment of silence and thus force me to listen to *their* favorite music while I am shopping, sitting in a waiting room, or "holding" on the telephone. (You know the world's controlled by the young when you listen to background music; whatever happened to melodies, rhapsodies, boogie-woogie, and the blues?)

9. PEOPLE I DON'T EVEN KNOW CALLING ME "TERESA." Now no one was more delighted than I to see "Have a nice day!" drop into oblivion (due, I like to think, to the fellow who consistently replied: "Thank you, but I have other plans"). However, I think I preferred it to the current fad, where everybody, regardless of age, profession, relationship, or status, is addressed by his/her first name. (I have often wondered if, in the unlikely event that President Reagan would ever stop at a drive-in bank to cash a check, the teller would hand him the cash and say: "Thank you, Ron!") While it rankles me to have teenagers or young adults I have never met call me "Teresa," I must admit that it bothers me even more to be called "Mrs. Bloomingdale" by friends who have known me forever, or who defer to my age when they aren't that much younger than I!

10. WINTER. I am referring here to winter in Nebraska, not Hawaii, Acapulco, or southwest Florida. I realize that God created snow and ice (though I can't imagine why) and that some people even enjoy the season, sledding, skiing, or skating. Aside from these slightly demented creatures, however, few people really relish winter—especially those of us who have a sixteen-year-old facing his/her first winter behind the wheel of our car.

11. DECIDING WHAT-TO-HAVE-FOR-DINNER-TO-NIGHT. It's such a little thing, isn't it? Then why does every mother in the world hate it so much? And why doesn't somebody do something about it? (You could be famous . . . revered . . . rich! Just figure out how to get somebody else to plan dinner tonight.)

12. MAGAZINE QUIZZES on such topics as "Are you and your spouse psychologically suited for each other?" or

"Do you truly try to understand your children?" or "Do you have the symptoms of this rare disease?" because I always seem to conclude "No" to the first two and "Yes" to the last.

But even more than magazine quizzes on marriage, motherhood, and diseases-I-just-know-I-have, I hate magazine articles promising quick cures just by doing something silly, like listing all the things you hate.

Frankly, I don't feel one bit better.

An Author's Guide to Obscurity

I've ordered an unlisted number
From unwanted calls I'll be free
In solitude curled
I'll be out of this world,
No bells will be tolling for me.

Of course, I have had to confide it
To that Unrefusable Few
Who have whispered it
(Though they denied it)
To, at least, four hundred and two.

3

AN AUTHOR'S GUIDE TO OBSCURITY

Like many authors and writers, I have an unlisted telephone number, and a lot of people want to know why. What makes us authors think we are so important we should have unlisted numbers?

My mother tells everybody that her daughter-the-author got an unlisted telephone number because "she was being bombarded with calls from her fans." I don't know what Mother considers a "bombard," but I had exactly six calls last month telling me how wonderful I am, and five of them were from Mother. (The sixth was from our son-at-college, who wanted to "borrow" twenty dollars. Remind me not to give him the unlisted number.)

My husband tells people that we got an unlisted number simply because we are tired of telling telephone salesmen that we don't need our carpets cleaned, our house painted, or our basement waterproofed, but that's only partially true; we *do* need our carpets cleaned, our house painted, and our basement waterproofed, but we *are* tired of lying about it.

My sister insists that I am just trying to avoid calls from fund raisers or nominating committees, but that's ridiculous. Fund raisers and nominating committees cannot be deterred by such simple obstacles as unlisted telephone numbers.

My daughter claims that we got our unlisted number because we were getting too many unwanted calls (to a sixteen-year-old, any call not for her is "unwanted"). But it would be more truthful to say I had to get an unlisted number because I was getting too many *wanted* calls.

Authors *are* bombarded with telephone calls, many of them from writers wanting to know how we managed to get our silly little books published while their Great American Novels continue to collect rejection slips. Now I love to talk to other writers, especially those who attribute to me any degree of expertise or wisdom, but my publishers were beginning to complain that I was spending too much time on the telephone and not enough time at the typewriter. (Publishers are funny people; they think that just because you tell them you will have your book finished by March, you actually will have your book finished by March.) So, to avoid temptation, I got an unlisted telephone number.

Though I am no longer allowed to chat with my fellow writers about this unpredictable business of publishing, I still feel an obligation to share the knowledge I have gained as the author of several published books. I am therefore dedicating this chapter to all you would-be authors who have read the many helpful how-to books on getting published but still feel there must be some secrets to which you have not been made privy. (There are.)

Following are questions you most often ask, with answers which will, I hope, guide you to another career, because God knows there are enough of us competing in this book business as it is.

Q. "How does one get a book published?"

A. Before sending your manuscript to an agent or publisher (or possibly even before writing the book) a would-be author would be wise to take a course in Acting (with emphasis on speech, gestures, clothing, and coiffure) and a course in Current Events, preferably something controversial. You should then contact an agent who can convince a publisher that you would be perfect on television, because no matter how good your book is, no publisher will buy it unless you are "talk show" material. This means that you must be either as beautiful as Bo Derek, as erudite as William F. Buckley, as funny as Phyllis Diller or as suave as Sir Laurence Olivier. (I have been on a lot of talk shows only because somebody mistyped my résumé. Actually, I am as beautiful as Bill Buckley, as erudite as Bo Derek, as suave as Ms. Diller, and as slapstick as Sir Laurence.) If a publisher can be persuaded that you are capable of matching wits with Johnny Carson or bouncing barbs off Phil Donahue, he will buy your book.

On the other hand, if you are as funny as Johnny or as caustic as Phil, maybe you should forget writing and go into television.

Q. "Do I need an agent?"

A. Yes, but the question is moot because no agent will want you unless you have already been profitably published, and if you have already been profitably published, why would you want an agent? Unfortunately, many publishers deal only with agents, so you are either going to have to get one or make one up, as my friend Greg did. After his book had been rejected (obviously unread) by more than a dozen publishers and agents, Greg had stationery printed with the title "Literary Agent" and submitted the manuscript again. It didn't sell, but when word got around that Greg was a "literary agent," he got so much business from other writers he gave up writing and moved to Florida, where he spends half the year lying on the beach reading manuscripts and the other half being wined-

and-dined by New York publishers. (He hit it rich when he contracted an author who had written a diet book for cats.)

Q. "Assuming that I cannot get an agent, is there any other way to break the publishing barrier and get my manuscript considered for publication?"
A. You might take the route many successful authors have taken, and that is to establish a friendship with somebody of real importance in the publishing industry.

Q. "You mean somebody like Nelson Doubleday or Michael Korda?"
A. No; I mean somebody like Norma Glutz.

Q. "Who's Norma Glutz?"
A. She's the junior "reader" whose job it is to sort through a million manuscripts, go "eenie-meenie-minie-mo," and send a favored few on to an editor.

Q. "If my manuscript is chosen for consideration, how long will I have to wait for a response?"
A. Forever, if you forgot to enclose a self-addressed stamped envelope; otherwise, it could be six days or six months. Amateur writers pray for a prompt reply, but the pros have learned that a quick response usually means a rejection. A lengthy wait, however, may indicate that your manuscript is undergoing thorough consideration. (On the other hand, it may mean that it is under a pile so deep Norma won't get to it till November.)

Q. "Should I use a pen name?"
A. Why? Are you on the lam?

Q. "Are author-publisher contracts difficult to read and interpret?"

A. Good heavens, no. All you need is a strong magnifying glass and a good lawyer. (If you don't read the contract until after you have signed it, you may also need a stiff drink.)

Q. "How are royalties paid?"

A. Reluctantly. Every six months the publisher will send you a financial statement listing all the sales of your book (domestic, foreign, subsidiary, etc.), the amount of money it has brought in, and the reasons why you aren't going to get any of it.

Q. "But if the book is selling, how could the author not get any money?"

A. This might best be explained by a memo I received recently from my own publisher, informing me that several chapters of my book had been purchased for reprint in an African magazine for a certain number of "rands." After conscientiously explaining the monetary exchange of rands into dollars, and offering hearty congratulations, the publisher included this parenthetical reminder: "The author receives, according to contract, a percentage of the money received by us. These payments are subject to foreign government taxes, transfer fees, and commissions." That was one of my better sales; it didn't cost me anything.

Q. "Just what is an 'autograph party'?"

A. A misnomer, that's what. Actually, every author has only one autograph party, and that's the first one, where her friendly neighborhood bookseller breaks out the champagne and sends out a thousand invitations to the author's friends, relatives, and neighbors, all of whom dutifully show up. From then on, the "autograph parties" are simply sessions where the author sits at a table in the middle of a book department, praying that somebody, *anybody,* will come by and buy a

book. This is often true for seasoned authors as well as begin-
ners, the sad fact being that even the most ardent of an author's fans hesitate to "impose" or "bother" an author with a
request for an autograph. Authors should not be concerned
about this seeming lack of interest, however (the reader will
buy the book, but just not while you're there), and you can
make good use of your time chatting with customers who stop
to ask directions to Better Dresses, the sweat sock sale, or the
rest room.

What is more embarrassing than having no one come to
your autograph party is having good, loyal friends come to
buy your book, and you can't remember their names. This
happens to me all too frequently. I have a terrible memory for
names, and have an awful tendency to draw a blank the moment a familiar face smiles at me and asks, "Would you autograph this personally, to me, please?" I was telling another
author about this, and he said, "There is a simple solution; you
simply ask them to spell their names for you. You could know
somebody for years, and not be expected to know how to spell
her name."

So I tried this, and it worked surprisingly well, until my last
autograph party when a very familiar woman walked up to
me, smiled, and said, "Congratulations, Teresa! Will you autograph your book, personally, for me?" I drew the expected
blank, but without a qualm I said:

"Of course, but tell me so I'll get it right; how do you spell
your name?"

She looked at me a moment and said, "P-A-T."

I swallowed, recovered, and said with a laugh, "Oh I know
that! I meant your *last* name!"

And she replied, "J-O-N-E-S."

Q. "What types of books sell best?"

A. Cookbooks and diet books (usually to the same customers).

Q. "How can an author help get his/her book on the bestseller list?"

A. There are three surefire ways to get your book on the best-seller list: (1) order fifty thousand copies of your book the first week it is out; (2) buy the New York Times Corporation and name yourself Book Editor; (3) change your name to Stephen King.

Q. "Does being an author make you famous?"

A. Only with your creditors.

And despite what that nasty man at the Credit Bureau says, that's *not* the reason I got an unlisted telephone number.

The Tube And I

(WITH APOLOGIES TO JOYCE KILMER)

I hope that I shall never see
Myself again upon TV.
When I was oh-so-sharply dressed,
Why did I photograph unpressed?
Must they insist upon a pose
Which called attention to my nose?
And was my conversation so corrupting
That someone had to keep on interrupting?
And
Since to weight I am so slightly tending
Do you really think it fair to catch me bending?
The next time I am asked to do a show,
I do hope it will be on radio.

4

THE TUBE AND I

If my complexion has turned a permanent shade of sickly green, it is because I have spent the past three weeks in Green Rooms.

Whether it be a luxurious lounge behind the scenes on a network television show, a tiny room inside a local radio studio, or just a chair offstage in a college auditorium, the place where "guests" wait their turn to go "before the cameras" or "on the air" or "on stage" is called the Green Room, and now I know why. Timid souls who are not accustomed to being "celebrities," and who are anxiously awaiting the moment when they must step into the spotlight and trade quips with a sophisticated "star" who *is* a celebrity, have a tendency to get queasy and turn green.

In the past month I have appeared on twenty-one television and radio talk shows, which means that I have served twenty-one "sentences" in green rooms, where I worried that I would trip over a cable, or miss the chair when I sat down, or talk out of turn, or develop an itch and inadvertently scratch, none of which I did, but all of which I *might* have done, which explains my current complexion of sickly green.

I am not a television-oriented person. I don't even spend much time on the outside looking in; God knows I'm not com-

fortable on the inside looking out. I'm not an actress or come-
dienne; I'm a writer. I wasn't trained to be a television person-
ality, and I certainly wasn't born to be one. If God had
intended for me to be a TV star, He would have made me
beautiful, or at least articulate, or at the very least, young.
Nothing makes one look, or feel, absolutely *old* as does appearing on television beside a gorgeous, glamorous talk-show host
who is so obviously *young,* or anyway is made up to look
young. (And if that makeup man can take ten years off Gary
Collins, why couldn't he do the same for me? Though I must
admit, he did try. What he didn't have to do was dance around
me waving that makeup brush and chanting: "What a challenge! I love a challenge!")

Since I am neither an actress nor a celebrity, why was I on
television? Because I am an author, and publishers now insist
that authors must not only write the book but help sell it as
well, and nothing sells a book better than a lively television or
radio talk show. In fact, if an author is not willing to go "on
tour," she or he might as well forget writing the book. I am
convinced that publishers would have passed up the Bible if St.
Paul hadn't been so good "on the road."

Doing television and radio talk shows may be easygoing for
such sophisticates as Joyce Brothers or Clare Boothe Luce, but
for a mediocre, middle-aged mother whose talents are limited
to winning arguments with her adolescent children and then
writing about same, appearing on network television or radio
(or even local television or radio) can be a terrifying experience.

Thus, when my publisher arranged for my very first TV
appearance, the producer insisted that I follow a script.

I said I didn't know that talk shows used scripts, and he
admitted that ordinarily they don't. In my case, however, they

thought it would be a good idea to tell me what to say, which was, of course, a nice way of telling me what *not* to say. The script they sent me was bright and witty and easy to memorize, so I set about doing so, line for line and cue for cue.

However, when the "big moment" finally arrived, and I was on the set in the television studio, sitting beside the talk show host and eagerly awaiting my cue, I realized to my horror that while I had carefully memorized that script, the host had not. In fact, no one had bothered to tell him of any script, and he was therefore understandably stunned when, on greeting me with "I'd like to welcome a wonderfully witty author and mother, Teresa Bloomingdale!" I responded by spluttering: "That's not what you were supposed to say!"

While I have since learned what to say on television talk shows, I have yet to learn where to look. I know I am supposed to look at the host; after all, it is to the host that I am talking, unless there is a studio audience, in which case it is acceptable to turn occasionally to them. It is even acceptable to look, however briefly, into the camera. Where it is *not* acceptable to look is at the monitor, that offstage television set that shows *you,* right there on TV, just like a star! I know I am not supposed to look at that monitor, but my eyes are drawn to it. It's like a pornographic picture; I know I shouldn't look at it; I don't want to look at it; but so help me I can't keep from looking at it! The host can be secretly signaling me to look at him; the producer can be wildly waving in the background, indicating that I should look at the host, but I don't; I look at me.

Because TV people are wonderful and tolerant and kind, they keep inviting me back, and I have been back, several times. But I have noticed that for my repeat performances, my chair has been turned more toward the host, and the monitor has been turned toward the wall.

I also have an awful time deciding what to wear on television. (I even have a hard time deciding what to wear on radio, which shows you how sophisticated I am in the field of performing arts.)

The first time I was to appear on television, to promote my book, *I Should Have Seen It Coming When the Rabbit Died,* my publisher cautioned that since my readers think of me as a rather rumpled, harried mother of ten, I should "go out and buy an outfit that would suit that role."

Go out and *buy* an outfit? What did they think I had in my closet? Halston originals?

Actually, I was tempted to buy something expensive and svelte for the occasion, but I decided that if everybody expected me to dress dowdy I would just have to dress dowdy. The only problem I had then was which of my dowdy dresses should I choose?

I finally settled on an old favorite, because its memories alone make me feel beautiful, and as I looked in the mirror I consoled myself with the thought that at least I would look as frumpy as the television producers evidently expected me to look.

I was to appear on a popular television show in Detroit. I was met at the airport by a cousin of my publisher, an absolutely gorgeous woman who had offered to act as my escort while I was in Detroit. She was (and still is, I presume) a stunningly beautiful woman: lovely features, stylish coiffure, elegant clothes. I knew she was ultra-stylish, because her stockings were the exact same shade as her designer suit. Even her makeup was magnificent: the right rouge, the perfect mascara, the subdued lip gloss—everything about the woman was stylish, sophisticated, and superb.

And to top it off, she had a marvelous sense of humor, a fact for which I was to be so very grateful. As she and I walked into the television studio, the producer of the talk show rushed to meet us, exclaiming: "Ah, Teresa Bloomingdale, I'd have recognized you anywhere; you look just like I pictured you!" . . . and brushed past me to greet my escort.

For one brief second I could see, flashing across that woman's face, the thought "My God, do I look like a mother of ten children?" but she laughed merrily and said, "Oh, no, *this* is Teresa; I'm just her driver!"

You can be sure that the next time Teresa appeared on television she was not wearing a dowdy dress. I didn't invest in a designer suit, but the one I did wear cost plenty, and it even had stockings to match!

I still have trouble deciding what to wear on television, though I know now that I should never wear white, nor should I wear bangle bracelets or necklaces that "make noise," for even the "swish" of a string of pearls is magnified by the microphone. Perhaps they should outfit guests from the costume room. At least that would avoid such embarrassing incidents as one I almost caused on "Hour Magazine."

When I heard that Gary Collins had invited me to be his guest on "Hour Magazine," I was ecstatic. Not only would I get to meet Gary Collins in person, I would also be given the opportunity to promote my book, *Up a Family Tree,* on one of the most popular talk shows in the country.

This time I really was determined to look stylish, for one cannot sit beside that handsome Gary Collins and look as if one has just come from cooking pot roast for twelve in a very cluttered kitchen, even if one just has! So I went out and bought myself a very elegant, very expensive brown wool suit. However, when I got it home, my husband took one look at it and said, "Take it back."

"I know, it's expensive . . ." I started to apologize, and he interrupted.

"It's not the expense that bothers me; it's the color, and the style. It's not feminine enough, for one thing, and for another thing, you should always wear blue."

"I do always wear blue," I said. (Do all husbands prefer blue?) "I'm sick of blue. I love this brown suit. Just feel this material; it's fantastic!"

"I don't care what material you wear," he said, "but I mean it about the color. Wear something blue; believe me, you look beautiful in blue."

"Oh, you think I'm beautiful in anything," I complained, but of course I took the brown suit back and exchanged it for blue, just in case he might be right. I bought an absolutely gorgeous blue Ultrasuede (well, he did say he didn't care what material I bought), and I have been forever grateful that I did. For when I walked onto the set of "Hour Magazine" and Gary Collins turned to greet me, I almost fainted when I saw what Gary was wearing. It had trousers instead of a skirt, but other than that it was exactly the same: my brown wool suit! Wouldn't it have been awful? We'd have looked like His and Hers.

But even Ultrasuede can be a catastrophe on TV. Since I had paid a small fortune for that suit, I naturally had to wear it everyplace, though even I had better sense than to wear it twice on television in the same town, or even in different towns, on the same day.

I did, however, think it would be safe to wear it two weeks after my appearance on "Hour Magazine" when I was a guest on the equally prestigious "Country Day" show out of Minneapolis.

What I did not realize was the fact that both shows had been taped for "later viewing," and (it could only happen to me) as luck would have it, they were both shown on Thanksgiving Day, one in the morning and one at noon.

My daughters wanted to know why I was so stupid as to wear the same outfit twice in one day; my sons wanted to know how I got from Minneapolis to Los Angeles so quickly, and my mother wanted to know why I was away from home on Thanksgiving Day.

And my sisters wanted to know how I conned my husband into buying me that Ultrasuede suit.

It wasn't easy. First you have to write a book. . . .

One would think that radio talk shows would be easier than television talk shows, since one does not have to worry about what clothes you should wear or what itch you can scratch. But this is not true; radio is much more difficult, because it is much more complicated. While a television studio may be cluttered with people—cameramen, producers, assistants, gofers—a radio studio is cluttered with equipment, all of which the talk show host seems to be responsible for. The television talk show host just sits back on a sofa and talks to you; the radio host talks to you while simultaneously working a dozen dials, taking telephone call-ins, accepting signals from the time-conscious producer, and frantically searching his paper-strewn desk for the next commercial, which is due to come up in three-seconds-two-seconds-one-second-NOW—and if somebody is in the middle of a sentence, the host must somehow finish it for him, *on time.* Radio talk show hosts are spectacular people; they truly can do ten things at once. (They'd make marvelous mothers.)

I have learned a lot about radio shows. For example, I now tell very, very short stories (to fit between the commercials); I have memorized the producer's signals (so I'll know when to speak and more important, when to shut up); and I have learned that most call-in questioners don't have a question at all, they just want to share a story, which is all too often funnier than mine. Do I mind this? Of course not, as long as they don't mind if I write it all down because on tomorrow's talk show, guess who's going to take credit for that story?

Of course, on television one must also be alert to signals, time, cues, etc.

In Cincinnati recently, I was on the "Bob Braun Show." Bob Braun has one of the most relaxed, easy, and enjoyable shows on TV, but I didn't realize just how easy and relaxed we all were until, during the preshow warm-up, when we were all laughing and teasing and talking, I turned to Bob and said, "When do they turn on the cameras?" and Bob laughed and said, "Teresa, they've just turned *off* the cameras; you've been on live TV for the past twelve minutes."

Throughout my literary career, I have appeared on almost one hundred television and radio talk shows, and while I have enjoyed them immensely, they may have ruined me as a writer. I am now so addicted to watching or listening to those fabulous talk shows, I can't find the time to write books.

It's a Great Place to Live

You may be a stray from Bombay
Or an orphan from Kalamazoo;
You may leave your palace
In Houston or Dallas
Because you are lonesome or blue.

You may feel you're a stranger in Maine,
Or you're catching a cold in Alaska,
You don't trust sunny Spain
(All that rain in the plain!)
So give us a try in Nebraska.

5

IT'S A GREAT PLACE
TO LIVE
BUT I WOULDN'T WANT
TO VISIT THERE

There is an ongoing joke among Nebraskans that New Yorkers know little or nothing about this great Cornhusker State, including its whereabouts.

I always thought the joke was a little silly, until I began working with various New York publishers, and one of them sent a bright young publicist to Omaha to interview me. As the publicist got off the airplane at Omaha's Eppley Field, she said:

"I can't believe we're here already; I always thought Nebraska was way over there on the other side of Oklahoma!"

I assumed she was kidding; surely *everybody* knows where Nebraska is! But evidently everybody doesn't, as we discovered during the 1982 Orange Bowl game, when NBC televised a map of the United States showing Nebraska directly south of North Dakota. Of course, it could be argued that they do, too, know where Nebraska is; they just don't know where South Dakota is.

Personally, I suspect that many New Yorkers tend to be confused, not just about South Dakota and Nebraska, but

about the entire Midwest. We Nebraskans are convinced that
New Yorkers look upon everything west of the Hudson River
as one vast prairie, broken only by a couple of oases called
Chicago and Las Vegas. They *are* clear about California, it
being the *other* civilized state, which, unfortunately, can only
be reached by flying over that vast expanse of prairie.

I know for a fact that back there (for reasons never explained to me, Nebraskans refer to New York as "back there,"
as opposed to Los Angeles, which is "out there") they consider
Cleveland a Midwestern city. Isn't that ridiculous? Everybody
else acknowledges the fact that Cleveland is in the East. If
New Yorkers think Cleveland is in the Midwest, where do they
think Omaha is? Probably "someplace over there by Cleveland."

While I will concede that many New Yorkers may be aware
of Nebraska's whereabouts, I am convinced that few of them
are clear about our lifestyle. Many New Yorkers think of Nebraska as "Indian territory," where we all live in "little houses
on the prairie," centering our lives around the corn harvest
and the cattle round-up, and going to bed each evening at dusk
because there isn't anything better to do and besides it saves on
candles and kerosene.

The fact that more than half a million Nebraskans live in
metropolitan Omaha, where we seldom see unshucked corn
and never see undressed beef, and where our evenings can be
spent at the symphony, the opera, the ballet, or the theater
(often preceded by a gourmet dinner at one of Omaha's famous restaurants), seems to be irrelevant, or even inconceiv-
able, to my buddies in the Big Apple.

When one of them visited me not long ago, she phoned first
to ask if she could fly into Omaha, or should she get off the
plane in Kansas City and arrange to drive the rest of the way?

(Thanks to Rodgers and Hammerstein, New Yorkers believe that "everything's up-to-date in Kansas City." Perhaps Omaha needs its own Broadway musical. On second thought, forget it. I shudder to think what it would be like.)

Another New York friend of mine, while visiting my family with her two children, told her five-year-old to "run outside and play in the sand hills." (May Mari Sandoz forgive me, but I have never seen Nebraska's famous Sand Hills, which are hundreds of miles from my home.) Before I could mention that little Lucy might find the Sand Hills rather far away for a playground (though after two days with little Lucy, I was tempted to take her outside and point her in that direction), Lucy's mother said, "It is safe for Lucy to play outside, isn't it? I mean, you don't have any problems with the Indians anymore, do you?"

I told her I had never had any problems with the Indians, since I had always stayed close to the stockade (as a matter of fact, the only Indians I ever saw were in South Dakota—wherever that is), but I was quite sure they had given up scalping for more mundane occupations. Furthermore, I said, most of Nebraska's Indians live in another part of the state.

"Oh, Jamie will be so disappointed," said my friend. "He did so want to see some Indians! Couldn't we drive across Nebraska so he could see the Indians, and the Sand Hills, and the prairie?"

Trying to convince a New Yorker that driving across Nebraska is comparable to driving from Manhattan to Montreal is impossible; they cannot believe that Nebraska is that big. But I got out of a tiring drive by telling her: "Sorry, we can't drive anyplace in Nebraska this weekend; the highways are closed at this time of the year because of the cattle drives."

Fortunately, she didn't suggest we round up a couple of horses and go watch.

I admit that Nebraskans love to tease Easterners about their misconceptions of our "pioneer" image. Some Nebraskans even relish the role. One such Nebraskan, a former governor who truly does look a little like a movie-conceived cowboy, particularly enjoys "playing the pioneer" when the occasion arises. On one occasion, this suave, sophisticated, and erudite governor was attending a conference at the Waldorf-Astoria in New York when he realized that two young people posted at the doors to give directions obviously considered him to be somebody "from the sticks." Rather than set them straight, he simply gave them a broad smile, then spoke loudly to his aide as they passed through the door, saying:

"Son, you're not gonna believe what they got in this here hotel—indoor privys! By golly, when we get back to Nebraska, I'm gonna order us one of them things for the statehouse!"

We have all heard New York referred to as "a great place to visit but I wouldn't want to live there." In like manner, Nebraska is often referred to as "a great place to live but I wouldn't want to visit there."

This bit of reverse psychology is perpetuated by a group of Nebraskans who, while admitting that this is the best state in the Union in which to reside, also claim that "there is nothing to do here." This is propaganda, pure and simple (or maybe impure and complex), because Omaha has everything from a nationally known art museum to an internationally renowned zoo. Why, then, do some Nebraskans "put down" our great state? Because they don't want to advertise what a good life we have in Nebraska, lest everybody in the United States decide to settle here. And while it is true that we have lots of space out here on the prairie, we can't be putting up every immigrant from east of the Hudson River who is looking for a better life!

As a consequence of our selfish attitude concerning this Cornhusker State, many Americans will never learn about Nebraska. Therefore, as an "alien" from Missouri who sneaked into Nebraska years ago and lived here ever since, I feel obliged to share some of the little-known facts about my adopted state.

1. Contrary to what they teach back there in New York, Nebraska is in the Midwest. It is not only in the Midwest, it's in the middle of the Midwest, though one might think, from glancing at a map of the United States, that it is in the middle of the country. Thus, we might assume that it is one of the Central States, but it isn't, for the simple reason that in the United States geography books there are no Central States. Traditionally, the United States is divided into the Southwest, West, Northwest, Northeast, East, Southeast, and South. Thus nobody knows exactly where Wisconsin, Minnesota, North Dakota, South Dakota, Nebraska, Iowa, Missouri, and Kansas are, except maybe for football fans, and as we say in Nebraska, who else matters?

2. Rodgers and Hammerstein will be interested to learn that "everything's up-to-date" in Nebraska cities, too. We have electricity, indoor plumbing, outdoor movies, dial telephones, and highways that go in both directions. (Which is more than you can say for the Connecticut Turnpike. I have a friend who rented a car in New York, intending to drive to New Haven for a Yale football game and return the following day to Manhattan. The last we heard from her, she was someplace in Nova Scotia, still headed north, still looking for an off-ramp.)

3. While it is true that many Nebraskans still live "on the prairie," their "little houses" are so enormous and elegant they make Southfork look absolutely squalid. Most Nebraskans, however, live in such metropolitan areas as Omaha, Lincoln, Bellevue, Grand Island, Scottsbluff, or, if it's a football Saturday, Memorial Stadium. ('Tis true; on a football Saturday, Memorial Stadium is the fourth largest "city" in Nebraska.)

4. Newcomers to Nebraska tend to think that much of the state is owned by Arabs, as so many places, businesses, and buildings bear the name Ak Sar Ben. Ak Sar Ben is not related to Abou Ben or any other Arab. It is simply "Nebraska" spelled backwards. (I know, but somebody's great-grandfather thought of it, and we're stuck with it. Nebraskans wouldn't dream of changing something their great-grandpas thought up, because many of those great-grandpas are still alive. In Nebraska, it's not only better, it's longer.)

5. Unlike our fellow countrymen who reside in New York ("New Yaw-wok"), people in Nebraska do not speak with an accent. In fact, we are probably the only people in the United States whose speech does not have any identifying characteristics. (No, we do *not* have a nasal twang; we just have a lot of hay fever.)

Lest you think I am prejudiced in favor of this great Cornhusker State, I will readily admit to one negative aspect: Nebraska's weather is bloody awful. The winters are very, very cold, and the summers are very, very hot. However, those two seasons are balanced by the other two. There is nothing to compare with spring and autumn in Nebraska. They are spectacular, inspiring, and beautiful days . . . both of them.

New York! New York!

I step a little higher when I'm there.
I stroll and hum the latest Broadway air.
In the windows that I pass,
My reflection in the glass
Assures me that I look quite debonair.

When I eat in the Big Apple.
Whether sauerkraut or scrapple,
They seem to turn the common into rare.
In their restaurants exclusive
They have flavors so elusive,
I say, in French of course, "Extraordinaire."

When I've heard the great Luciano,
Liberace at piano,
And Nureyev has thrilled me with ballet;
When my Visa card some morning

Issues stern and solemn warning,
I wonder how I'll pass the coming day.

I'll just go out and walk and gawk.
The place to do it is New Yawk!

6

NEW YORK! NEW YORK!

If a New Yorker's notions of Nebraska are ill-conceived, so are a Nebraskan's notions of New York, or more specifically, *this* Nebraskan's notions of New York.

While many Nebraskans go to New York frequently, I am not one of them. In fact, until last spring, I had never been there at all, and with good reason. I was too chicken. I knew what went on in New York! Hadn't I seen *The Out-of-Towners* three times? New York City is a glass and steel jungle where you can't see the sky because of the tall buildings, and you never see a tree because there aren't any (except for those in Central Park, and that one that grows in Brooklyn). You dare not drive in Manhattan because the traffic moves so fast it's downright dangerous, and you dare not walk in Manhattan because you might get mugged. Oh, I knew all about New York, with its high-priced hotels and excessive cab fares and expensive restaurants. No siree, I wasn't about to go someplace where I would be ripped off, if not rubbed out!

So when my editor called last spring to invite me to New York for editorial conferences, intermingled with some sightseeing and a couple of evenings-on-the-town, I told her to forget it.

"Do you think I'm crazy?" I asked her. "I'm not about to visit the crime capital of the world! I'd be scared out of my shoes every minute I was there!"

"Don't be silly, Teresa," she said, "people come to New York every day! Some of us even live here! Bring your husband with you, if you want, but do come, because we have to sit down and go over promotion plans for your next book."

No author can afford to let her publishers off the hook when they agree to discuss promotion plans for one of her books, so I agreed to go to New York.

My husband, however, didn't.

"Are you crazy?" he asked me. (He had seen *The Out-of-Towners* five times.) "Why would you want to go to New York? Nobody goes to New York unless they have to!"

"Well, I have to," I said, and told him about the meetings concerning my new book.

"But I don't have to," he said. "In fact, I can't. I've got conferences scheduled all that week. Why don't you take one of the kids with you?"

"I may be crazy," I said, "but I'm not that crazy. How would I explain to the rest of the kids that I am taking one of them? And which one should I take?"

"Mary, of course," he said. "She's the only one who has the required qualification."

"What's that?" I asked.

"Enough money to pay her own way," he said. "Furthermore, since she has been doing so much secretarial work for you, she is the logical person to accompany you."

So we broached the subject to Mary, and of course she was thrilled at the prospect of seeing New York, despite the fact that she would be encumbered by a mother.

After a brief hassle with her college profs to reschedule her spring exams, and a lengthy hassle with her father to restock her spring wardrobe ("You don't really expect me to wear *these* in New York! They'd die laughing!"), Mary and I were ready to make our first trip to Manhattan.

As my husband drove us to the airport, he rattled off typical husband-father rules: "Don't walk down Broadway after dark . . . don't walk in Central Park anytime . . . don't walk anyplace alone; stick together . . . don't spend too much money . . . don't be intimidated by those smart, sophisticated New Yorkers; they're not any brighter than you are . . ." (God help them) . . . "and watch out for hijackers! I don't like for you to fly!"

I don't like to fly either, but it's not hijackers I'm concerned about; it's *gravity*. I used to worry that the plane would crash; lately I find myself worrying that it won't come down at all. Since I heard just how high these airliners go, I cannot zoom into the wild blue yonder without wondering if we are going to zoom just a bit too high, right out of gravity's clutches, where we will be doomed to orbit the earth forever. Frankly, I don't mind dying, but I dread the thought of spending the rest of my life circling the globe with nothing to break the monotony but another thawed turkey-burger and a teensy bottle of bourbon. There are worse things than being hijacked.

To Mary's disappointment, we didn't get hijacked ("Haven't you always wanted to see Havana?"), and to my relief, the plane soon began to descend for landing at La Guardia. From the moment the airplane banked over New York harbor, both of us fell in love with Manhattan.

As I saw the Statue of Liberty for the first time, and looked over the famous Manhattan skyline, two of my Manhattan misconceptions were shattered: the Lady Liberty faces the sea; why had I always assumed she was waving to us on shore?

And Manhattan Island is tiny! I have always thought of it as huge! In fact, Manhattan Island is only about one-third the area of Omaha; how could so many millions live and work here?

As we drove into midtown Manhattan, it became obvious that many, *many* millions are here, for at any intersection at least two million are trying to cross the street, and another million are trying to hail cabs.

Our cab driver disposed of another of my misconceptions. He was cautious and courteous, but the fare was relatively inexpensive. (His "relatives" being in Nebraska, where it cost me more to get from my home to Eppley Field than it did to get from La Guardia to midtown Manhattan.)

As my misconceptions of Manhattan vanished, so did my promises to my husband. Despite his warnings about robbers and muggers, Mary and I walked everyplace, sometimes together, sometimes alone, depending on our destination. (I wanted to shop at Saks; she wanted to go to the museum; I wanted to see the view from the Empire State Building; she wanted to watch the trading at the stock exchange; I wanted to see the Rockettes dance at Radio City Music Hall; she wanted to listen to the delegates argue at the United Nations. There's no accounting for the tastes of this younger generation!)

We walked everyplace because everybody walks in New York, especially in the springtime. We even walked through Central Park and loved every inch of it. True, it was daylight when we took that stroll from the Tavern on the Green across the park to Bloomingdale's, but it was almost midnight when we walked down Broadway, after seeing Lauren Bacall in *Woman of the Year*, in fact we walked all the way back to our hotel, along with hundreds of other theatergoers, none of whom seemed to be concerned about possible assault.

Broadway broke another misconception: Why had I thought the Palace would be the ultimate in theaters? It is neither as large nor as lavish as Omaha's Orpheum, and while both the play and the acting were superb, they were no more professional than productions I have seen at the Omaha Community Playhouse. (Though I later learned the reason for this. When I mentioned the comparison to a Broadway producer, he said, "But the Omaha Playhouse is famous, not just for producing such prominent actors as Henry Fonda, Dorothy McGuire, and Marlon Brando, but also for the international awards it has won under the present director, Charles Jones!" Geoff Jones's dad is famous? Why didn't I know that!)

In the few days we were there, Mary and I saw almost every "sight" in Manhattan, from the Battery to Harlem, from the East River to the Hudson. We prayed in St. Patrick's, peeked into the Plaza and the Pierre, walked through the Waldorf (which is about all one can afford to do at the Waldorf), and shopped in "our" store, Bloomingdale's, where Mary tried to spoil my fun by admitting to the clerk that "this Mrs. Bloomingdale is Teresa, not Betsy" (though it made no difference; he had never heard of either one of us) and where I broke the last of my promises to my husband: I spent a lot of money. And wouldn't you, if half the items in the store were imprinted with your name?

The only frustrations we found in Manhattan concerned the restaurants; there are too many of them. One can spend an entire evening just trying to decide where to eat. And once you decide, no matter how excellent the food or elegant the decor, you will wonder if someplace else might have been even better.

Such was my dilemma our first night in New York. After being honored by Doubleday at a cocktail party in their Fifth Avenue suite, I was asked if I wanted to go to dinner at "21," or would I, perhaps, prefer the Four Seasons? After much discussion, we decided on the Four Seasons, and it was truly magnificent. The cuisine was exceeded in elegance only by the decor. We thoroughly enjoyed that dinner, and to this day I crave yet one more taste of that chocolate torte!

The next morning we discovered that had we decided to dine at "21," we would have shared the evening with former President Richard Nixon and his charming wife Pat.

"Too bad you missed President Nixon," teased my editor as she read the item in the morning paper, whereupon my daughter quickly replied, "Too bad President Nixon missed Mom!" (And this from my greatest critic! The rumors are right; Manhattan does have a magical effect on people.)

Mary tells me now that I seem to remember nothing of New York but the meals; that's not true, but if it were, it would be understandable. The restaurants in Manhattan are truly special, whether you are brunching at the Barclay-Intercontinental, having a leisurely lunch at the Top of the Sixes or in the Tavern on the Green, dining in style at the Four Seasons, or finger-eating pizza at that fabulous little place on Seventh Avenue off Broadway.

We had a wonderful time in New York, but I must admit that I was embarrassed by my ignorance of the town and its people. So for those of you who have similar misconceptions about New York, and who may be planning your first visit to the Big Apple, I offer the following information:

1. New York has both sky and trees; incredible but true. Of course, many of the trees are now *inside* the buildings, which I think is sad. I mean, how would *you* like to be a tree who "lifts its leafy arms to pray," and instead of looking at God all day, sees only Waldenbooks on the Second Level?

2. It is perfectly safe to drive in Manhattan, providing you aren't going anyplace, because not only does the traffic not speed, it doesn't even move. However, while it is not dangerous to drive, it is definitely unwise, because in the unlikely event that you do reach your destination, you won't be able to find a place to park. (Unless perhaps you own a parking lot, and after you have paid the first hour's fee in one, you'll think you do.)

3. It is also safe to walk in New York. When I asked my editor about a recent mugging on Fifth Avenue, she explained that the muggee had been wearing a highly publicized diamond necklace. Therefore, if you are going to walk in New York, it's a good idea to leave all of your diamond necklaces at home.

4. Before you agree to walk anyplace, find out where you are headed. "It's only twenty blocks!" may sound exhausting to a tourist from the Midwest, where a block is a *block* (and usually uphill), but in Manhattan the streets are so close together you could hopscotch from corner to corner. Not so the avenues; the avenues are so far apart the "next corner" may be over the horizon. So if you are headed north or south, walk; if you're going east or west, take a taxi.

5. Walking in Manhattan is dangerous only if you try to cross a street (or avenue). You see, nobody in New York knows about traffic lights. Oh, they have them; they just don't know what they are for. Neither the drivers nor the pedestrians seem to understand that "red" means "stop" and "green" means "go." To them, everything means "go." (If we drove or jay-walked like that in the Midwest, we'd be either dead or in jail.) So avoid crossing any streets. This may seem a bit confining at first, but you'll soon realize that Manhattan is so compressed, you can easily spend most of your vacation (and all of your money) in one square block.

6. If you decide to take a taxi (you will quickly note that there are more taxis in Manhattan than there are people), the acceptable method of hailing a cab is simply to throw yourself on the street in front of it. (This explains why there are fewer people in Manhattan than there are taxis.)

7. Despite the fact that there seem to be a zillion cars on the streets of Manhattan, most people who live or work there walk. This is why all the women you see are dressed in designer suits and sneakers. Once in the office they take off their sneakers and put on pumps, and at five o'clock they reverse the procedure. This practice alone proves that New Yorkers are smarter than we are.

8. If this is your first trip to the "big city," have no fear that native New Yorkers will look down their noses at you because you are from a "small town" (which, to New Yorkers, is anyplace other than New York). They won't, and for one simple reason: *there are no native New Yorkers.* True, some people are born in Manhattan, but when they grow up they move to Minneapolis or Miami. As for those people who currently reside in Manhattan, they came from Oregon, or Kansas, or Ohio, or Pennsylvania—in other words, from the Midwest (which, you will remember, is everything east of the Hudson River).

Both Mary and I fell in love with New York, and we agreed that it is not only a great place to visit, but we'd love to live there! I think I could be very happy living in Manhattan, maybe in a condominium overlooking Central Park, or perhaps in a penthouse apartment in the Pierre, or even just a simple suite in the Waldorf Towers. Though, as Mary reminded me, we wouldn't want to spend weekends or summers in the city, so of course we should also have a seaside home in the Hamptons!

Well, of course!

A Hoagie is a Carmichael . . .

I am lost in the new generation
Though I'm raising a bevy of ten,
Without reservation
What they call conversation
Quite simply, is out of my ken.

But they stand in a line and accuse me
Of speaking a language that's strange.
They insist it's a slur
When I always refer
To my counter-top stove as a "range."

I should get a bilingual sitter,
And try, in spite of the cost,
For a meeting of minds
(With the aid of some signs),
Lest my new generation get lost.

7

A HOAGIE
IS A CARMICHAEL . . .
NOT A SANDWICH!

When my nephew Kevin was in kindergarten, he came home from school one afternoon and announced that he flunked a word-picture quiz because he had identified a "refrigerator" as an "icebox" and the teacher had marked it wrong.

My sister called the teacher to argue the point, and was surprised to discover that the teacher (age twenty-two) had never heard of an icebox.

That's the trouble with the modern generation; they don't speak English. They are so "into" such Americanisms as "microwaves," "woks," "photoelectric-image-converters," and "digital chronometers" they don't know what we're talking about if we refer to a "stove," a "skillet," a Brownie camera," or "the big-and-little-hands of a clock."

Not long ago my mother was here for dinner and in the course of the conversation referred to a "nickelodeon."

"What's a nickelodeon, Grandma?" asked my daughter, and my mother explained that a nickelodeon was "like a jukebox, but took nickels rather than dimes or quarters." Whereupon my eldest son said he'd never heard of the term "jukebox" and

my youngest claimed he'd never seen a "nickel." (I reminded
him that a nickel is the change he is supposed to bring home
from his hot lunch money but never does; perhaps he leaves it
on the counter, feeling it's not worth carting home—an attitude I used to have about mills.[1])

I don't know why my children are so ignorant of words
indigenous to my generation. When I was their age, I always
knew what my mother meant when she referred to the Vic-
trola, the davenport, chiffoniers, or galoshes, even though they
had long since been replaced by a phonograph, the sofa, bu-
reaus, and boots.

We who were children in the thirties and forties made every
effort to understand our parents' vocabulary, not only because
it was expected that we "speak their language" but also because we never could have passed those archaic literature
courses had we not known the meaning of such terms as
"drawing room,"[2] "smoking jacket,"[3] "pinafores,"[4] or "por-
ticoes."[5]

In an effort to educate those of you who speak only Young
American and are burdened with Olde Englishe parents, I offer here a brief vocabulary list of words you may hear in the
unlikely event that you should stay at the dinner table long
enough to say something other than: "Sorry-I'm-late-pass-the-
catsup-good-dinner-Ma-may-I-be-excused?"

[1] A quarter-size, lightweight coin, ten-to-the-penny, necessary when every nickel was
taxed one mill. Went out with the nickel.
[2] A fancy living room; nobody "drew" anything, except maybe a scowl from a dis-
pleased parent. (Which was unlikely, as kids weren't allowed in drawing rooms.)
[3] What Daddy wore around the house so he wouldn't burn holes in his suit coats with
cigar ashes.
[4] Also called "apron"—a garment worn by mothers in the days before the Golden
Arches, the Colonel, or takeout pizza.
[5] A porch. (A patio with a roof!)

ANTIMACASSAR. Small cloth placed on the back of sofa to protect the upholstery from hair oil.[6] Went out of style because Dad kept knocking it behind the sofa and cursing. Replaced by slipcovers.

SLIPCOVERS. Unlike the antimacassar (antimassacar? Maybe it went out of style because nobody could spell it . . . or pronounce it!) which protected only a portion of the upholstery, the slipcover protected the entire piece. So called because they could be easily "slipped" on,[7] slipcovers were placed on the new furniture the day it was purchased and kept thereon until the room was redecorated and the furniture replaced by new pieces, which were, of course, immediately covered with new (or possibly the same) slips. Which explains why husbands asked, "Honey, why did you spend six months choosing 'just the right material' for a sofa nobody can see?" And now-grown children say, "I'm sorry, Mama, but I honestly cannot remember the red velvet chairs you say sat in your living room for twenty years!" The only furniture that was not slipcovered was the furniture in the parlor.

PARLOR. The most lavishly furnished but least-used room in the house; always at the front of the house.[8] The parlor was used only for entertaining important guests or waking[9] deceased relatives. Modern homes still have lavishly furnished "front rooms" but nobody knows why, as even the most important guests are entertained in the much more comfortable

[6] Nature's own hair-conditioner; disappeared when kids began shampooing six times a day.

[7] Only they couldn't; you had to tug and pull like crazy.

[8] So that passing neighbors, on glancing through the front window, would think the whole house was that luxurious.

[9] So called because the mourners stayed up all night to "watch" the body. (Why? Did they think it would run away?)

family room, and dead relatives are always waked at the mortuary.[10]

REC ROOM. A room, usually in the basement,[11] where little children played with their toys and older children played Ping-Pong or pool or records on their automatic record players. Went out of style because many kids thought it was a "wreck room" and treated it accordingly. Replaced by day care centers and computer arcades.

BEAU. Any young man courting[12] your daughter. (More than a boy friend, not quite a fiancé.)

GOING STEADY. A relationship between a boy and girl in which they both agreed not to date others. To a girl, "going steady" meant eternal love, absolute faithfulness, a prelude to marriage. To a boy, "going steady" meant going noplace—literally. Instead of taking her dining or dancing, they could now just sit on her front porch and spend the evening necking[13] and maybe even petting.[14]

BEING PINNED. A relationship indicating the couple was "engaged to be engaged," symbolized by his presenting her with his fraternity pin, which she then wore constantly, even on her pjs.[15] Went out of style when boys began to say: "A ring? Whaddya want a ring for? You've already got my fraternity pin!"

[10] More expensive but certainly less exhausting.
[11] So their parents wouldn't hear them.
[12] Dating; had nothing to do with courts, unless they played a lot of tennis.
[13] Approved hugging and kissing.
[14] Unapproved hugging and kissing.
[15] Pajamas.[16]
[16] A garment worn in bed at night.

CHASTE. What young lovers were before they were married.[17]

ROMANCE. A love affair in which young lovers reveled in each other's company, got to know each other's likes and dislikes, hopes and dreams, goals and ambitions, without worrying about "Your place or mine?"[18]

THE LITTLE BLACK BOOK. A small, well-worn address book carried by boys to impress their girl friends (and worry their mothers). The Little Black Book supposedly listed the phone numbers of gorgeous girls anxiously awaiting his phone call; it actually listed numbers he copied out of the sorority handbook, few of which he ever got up the courage to call.

A ZOOT SUIT. A man's suit featuring extra-long jacket, excessively wide shoulders, and peg-leg pants; incorrectly remembered as the "uniform" of the "hip"[19] young man of the forties. Actually worn only by musicians who were paid to push the song of the same name (and one weird kid I knew who played sax in the school band and considered himself "cool"[20]).

BOOGIE-WOOGIE. A percussive style of blues-on-piano, noted for its steady bass beat. Not composed (as your grandfather claimed) for the sole purpose of driving parents crazy. Boogie-woogie, sometimes compared to the earlier ragtime

---

[17] Misdefined by some modernist big mouths as "Chaste: girls who aren't chased."

[18] Differed from "an Affair," in which lovers reveled in each other's company, while constantly worrying that a spouse would find out about it.

[19] "Hip" or "hep" meant "with it," "up to date," "interested in the newest developments" (especially Helen Sermanski's).

[20] a/k/a "hip" or "hep"; see 19.

and the later rock 'n' roll,[21] was marvelous music that made its listeners lighthearted, carefree, and gay.[22]

JITTERBUG. A jazz-type dance in which couples swung, twirled (and sometimes threw) their partners in vigorous acrobatics. (Yes, children, your father and I did the jitterbug, and if you think we looked ridiculous, you should have seen your grandparents doing the bunny hop! Or yourselves, doing the New Wave!)

JALOPY. A very old, extremely dilapidated automobile, highly revered by teenage drivers of the forties (probably because they never got to drive anything else[23]). Despite their disreputable appearance, jalopies were approved by parents because (a) jalopies couldn't go fast enough to break the speed limit, and (b) jalopies were seldom involved in accidents. (Who'd know?)

ROADSTER. The precursor to the convertible; the roadster was coveted by all, especially roadsters with rumble seats.[24]

STREETCAR. What those of us who didn't own an automobile rode to school.[25] A streetcar ran on rails, like a train, but only within the city, like the present-day bus.[26]

---

[21] Ridiculous comparisons; one could *dance* to boogie-woogie! (See "Jitterbug".)

[22] In the forties and fifties, "gay" had no sexual connotation whatsoever, and while I am absolutely and totally without prejudice, I could cheerfully (gaily!) kill the guy who stole "gay"!

[23] Except for Alfie Adams, who drove a Hudson, but what can you expect of a kid who went to Andover?

[24] A seat that opened from the back of the roadster, thus turning a two-seater into a thirteen-passenger vehicle.

[25] Except, of course, for those days when we "walked ten miles to school in snow up to our elbows."

[26] A city-run passenger vehicle, ridden by fathers who let their kids con them out of their car.

PEDAL-PUSHERS. Calf-length slacks concocted for girls who (a) rode bicycles a lot or (b) had neat ankles.

THE CHESTERFIELD COAT. A tailored coat with a velvet collar, which, in 1946, every single sixteen-year-old girl "had to have or simply die!"[27]

CHAPERONE. The unlucky person who got conned into accompanying unmarried couples on weekend ski trips.

HANKY-PANKY. That which did not take place on weekend ski trips due to the omnipresent chaperone.

ROADHOUSE. An out-on-the-highway restaurant-bar, popular with college kids because it provided a dance floor (with Hit Parade jukebox), watered-down drinks (allowing us to be both sophisticated and sober), and tables long enough, or booths big enough, for the entire gang to gather around and talk, argue, or exchange ideas far into the night. (Sometimes even till midnight!) Roadhouses were unpopular with parents because of the "dim lighting," "suggestive music" ("To spend one night with you . . . in our old rendezvous . . ." Come to think of it, maybe some of those songs were suggestive; I wonder why we didn't think so at the time?) and "cheek-to-cheek dancing." (How else could six couples dance on a four-by-four floor?)

I was going to dedicate this chapter to my nephew Kevin, who, as a child, was such a good little kid. He pleased his parents, acknowledged his old Aunt Teresa (even when he was with friends!), even spoke our language. But something must have happened to him. Just the other night I was driving past

---

[27] While some sixteen-year-olds may have died in the year 1946, it is safe to say that none of them died for lack of a chesterfield coat, for in the winter of 1946, absolutely every sixteen-year-old girl was wearing one.

one of those "open-air" New Wave nightclubs, and who should I see on the dance floor, flopping like a scarecrow to music that would make Mick Jagger shudder, but Kevin! I couldn't believe it! Wouldn't you think that a kid who knows an icebox when he sees one would have the decency to take his date to a roadhouse?

The Camera Lies

The girls all cried that they would "look just awful!"
The boys complained because I cut their hair.
The little ones said it should be unlawful;
That washing up for pictures is unfair.

Now I regret ignoring all their strictures.
The proofs are back and I am quite distressed.
There are only strangers posed in all these pictures;
I don't recognize my children cleaned and pressed!

8

THE CAMERA LIES

"Since all the kids will be here for Christmas this year," mused my husband last December, "let's have a family picture taken."

"Let's don't," I said firmly, and passed him a forbidden slice of French bread in an attempt to distract him from such a diabolical idea.

"Why not?" he asked. "Wouldn't you like to have an updated picture of the family?"

"I'd love to have an updated picture of the family," I admitted, "but I am too old for it."

"Too old?" he chided, "don't be silly. Anyway, you are quite photogenic, your pictures always make you look younger than you really are."

"Thanks a lot," I said sarcastically, and I grimaced as I glanced at my most recent portrait, currently displayed on the dining room buffet where, in lieu of a sterling silver coffee service or tea set, we feature family photographs. "Just look at that picture of me; I look like somebody's grandmother."

"But, Teresa," laughed my husband, "you *are* somebody's grandmother!"

"That's not the point!" I argued. "One can *be* a grandmother and not *look* like a grandmother! When I first saw the proofs for that picture I thought they were of my mother! I refuse to believe I look that old; and don't tell me the camera doesn't lie. That one did!"

"You're the one who mentioned being too old to have your picture taken," said my husband, "not I."

"I didn't mean I'm too old to get *my* picture taken," I said. "I meant I'm too old to have a family picture taken. You're just a father; you don't have any idea what a mother has to go through to get her children's picture taken."

I would be willing to bet that there isn't a mother alive who wouldn't rather rely on her memory than endure the ordeal of trying to capture for posterity images of her children in a well-planned portrait.

If they didn't have to be "well-planned" or a "portrait," it might be different. Though taking candid snapshots can be traumatic, too, especially if Himself insists that the kids be neat and clean and on time. Personally, my favorite photos of our kids are those taken "to finish the roll." After gathering everybody around the Christmas tree, and catching everybody in their Easter attire, a summer project will be to "get those films developed, will you, honey?" which means I have to use up the last few pictures on the roll. And that's when we would get the best pictures, like the baby in the high chair, splattered with cereal and screaming to be "let down!" . . . or the toddler on his trike, racing around the driveway trying to run over the dog . . . or the ten-year-old, caught in the cookie jar . . . or the six-foot-two teenager snoozing on the lawn chaise while the mower idles beside him, patiently awaiting another lap around the yard. But do I have these favorite photos on display? Of course not! I have, instead, a carefully planned studio portrait that took me three weeks to get ready for and three more to recover from and doesn't bring fond memories of my children because it doesn't look like them.

I well remember the day that picture was taken. The only one who was in a good mood was the photographer, who, in a spirit of goodwill (and influenced, no doubt, by the thought of what ten children, all under the age of sixteen, would do to his studio) had offered to take the picture in our home. I had happily accepted his offer before I realized that this would mean that I would have to clean up the house as well as the kids.

But the house could wait. First I had to rehabilitate the kids. I lined them all up in the living room and issued instructions.

"The photographer is coming Saturday," I said, "so I want all of you to be here at exactly one o'clock, not one minute later. You will dress in the clothes I choose for you, and I expect you to be clean and neat. This means, of course, that you boys will have to get haircuts."

"A haircut!" yelled my eldest son, whose proudest achievement of that year was getting his hair to grow to a then-fashionable shoulder length. "I'll run away before I get a haircut!"

"You can run away after you get the haircut—and after we get the picture taken," I said. "Till then, consider yourself still enslaved, and do as you are told. On Friday afternoon you and your younger brothers will go to the barber to be shorn—and tell him I want to see your ears! And for heaven's sakes, wash your ears before you go—if you can reach them under that tangled mass."

"You think our hair is tangled," cried my younger son; "just look at the girls'!"

"I know," I said with a sigh, and contemplated the waist-length hair of my nine-year-old. How could she possibly get such tangles? Now my four-year-old daughter's tangles were understandable; in lieu of thumb-sucking, she sought "security" in winding her curls around her finger, and around and around and around again, and sometimes up and under, into knots a sailor would envy. I mentally set aside all of Friday morning just to disentangle, brush, shampoo, and curl my daughters' crowns of glory in preparation for their portrait.

"Now for clothes," I continued my instructions, "Jim will wear Mike's blue blazer, and Mike can wear John's brown sport coat, and John should just about fit into Lee's gray suit." (Only a mother of multiples can understand how, when it comes to "dress-up" time, everybody usually resorts to a hand-me-downs.)

"And as usual, Lee gets the new clothes!" complained Lee's younger brother. "He's your favorite!"

"He's not my favorite!" I shouted (knowing full well that years hence he would remind me that he was "never your favorite!") "He gets the new clothes because he's the oldest!"

"Other families don't do it that way!" cried another younger son.

"Other families don't have seven sons!" I countered. "Now please, kids, try to be more cooperative. After all, it isn't every day you get your picture taken." (Fortunately, it isn't even every year.)

The designated time arrived, and to my surprise, seven of my ten children showed up to greet the photographer. (Take it from one who knows; seven out of ten is considered success.)

"Where is your sister?" I asked my five-year-old Peggy as I reached down to pull up her lagging knee-length socks.

"She's in her room," said Peg. "She says she's not coming down until she has to; she's mad 'cause you made her wear that 'little girl' dress." (What else would you make a nine-year-old wear?)

"Go tell her to come down," I said, "and tell Mike and Jim to get down here, too."

"They're not here," said John. "They rode off on their bikes a few minutes ago. They said they'd be right back. Do you want me to go find them?"

"No!" I said. "The last time I sent you to look for somebody I had to send somebody to look for you. Here, hang up this jacket and put these magazines away! I just cleaned up this room this morning!"

"Mom," interrupted my six-year-old Danny, "can I take off my shoes? They hurt my feet."

"I know, Danny," I said sympathetically, "and I promise to buy you new shoes tomorrow. You grow too fast!"

Eventually Jim and Mike returned, all sweaty and wind-blown, which meant the photographer had to wait for them to freshen up. Mary reluctantly appeared in her "little girl" dress, and she was right; she looked ridiculous. Why hadn't I realized how much she had grown since Easter? So we had to take time out while we scrounged around for another dress for Mary, one which, if she leaned over a little, looked almost the right length.

We finally got everybody in place, and the photographer paused a moment, looked puzzled, and said:

"Is there any particular reason why that child is not wearing shoes?"

"Of course there is!" I said, "he is just a baby; he can't even walk yet. Why would he need shoes?"

"I'm not referring to the baby," said the photographer. "I'm talking about that kid there!" And he pointed to Danny, who was standing self-consciously by the sofa, in stocking-feet.

"Danny, where are your shoes?" I asked.

"I don't know! I took them off for just a minute and they disappeared!"

"That's okay," said the photographer, "we'll just have Danny stand behind the sofa. Is it okay if I pull it out from the wall?"

"Of course," I said. "Boys, give him a hand."

They pulled the sofa away from the wall and uncovered a baseball bat, a school sweater, two comic books, three popsicle sticks, one-half of a peanut butter sandwich, and no fewer than five absolutely filthy sweat socks.

"I'm terribly sorry about this," I told the photographer as I scooped up the debris. "I did clean this room, but that was this morning!"

"No problem!" he said cheerfully. "Maybe we should leave it; make the picture more realistic!"

"I don't want realism!" I said. "I want a picture of my children looking neat, clean, and happy!"

And that's exactly what we got: a portrait of ten well-groomed, carefully coiffured children all saying "cheese." I was thrilled with the picture, until I sent a print to my mother and she wrote to me saying: "What beautiful children! Whose are they?"

That was ten years ago, and since then I have relied on the picture man who takes the annual school photos. Since he must photograph about four hundred children in an afternoon, he has no time to fret about unwashed faces or uncombed hair; consequently, those pictures of my children are precious to me.

However, I agree with my husband that the time has come for another family picture, and while I know that he expects me to see to it that his kids are dressed-to-the-nines, looking sharp, sophisticated, and covered with smiles, I am planning a secret compromise. After the photographer has snapped the last well-planned "sitting," and the boys have loosened their ties, the girls have kicked off their shoes, and everybody has returned to their favorite hangout, the kitchen, I am going to ask the photographer to "finish his roll."

You can bet their grandma will recognize *those* kids, and I'll bet that becomes our favorite family photograph!

Show and Sell

Leonard and Bonnie's kids are gone;
There's a realty sign sitting out on their lawn,
And they've moved to a bungalow.

Will they miss the patter of little feet?
And the big old house that was hard to heat?
I asked, and they said "No."

But their kids have seen the futility
Of paying both rent and utility,
And want to come back for a spell.

So I asked my good friends Bonnie and Len,
"Isn't it nice to have the kids home again?"
And they said: "Go to hell."

9 ∾

SHOW AND SELL

"What are we going to do with this house when we're through with it?" mused my husband as we relaxed in our living room after an exhausting afternoon packing one more child off to college.

"What makes you think we'll ever be through with it?" I asked.

"Well, Peg is the seventh of our brood to leave home," he said, though I wondered why he thought going off to college was leaving home.

"Yeah," I reminded him, "and Mike is the third to move back again. Mike said it was just for a couple of months, till he could find an apartment, but Jim said the same thing when he came home from the Marines. That was three years ago, and Jim's still camping out in the basement."

"It's your fault the kids keep coming back," said my husband. "You lure them home with gourmet meals, then keep them here with promises of laundry facilities and free shampoo, because you can't bear the thought of an empty nest."

He's right. I do dread the day when we'll have an empty nest, but having the kids all gone has nothing to do with it. I dread an empty house, but not because I won't know what to do with myself; I dread it because I won't know what to do with the house. Or to be more truthful, I *will* know what to do with it, which is sell it, and frankly I admit that I share the dream of every homeowner, which is to live in the house we own until I am carried out of it, feet first, and can leave the problem of what-to-do-with-the-darn-place to my reluctant heirs.

The first time my husband and I had to sell a home was years ago when the kids were little. We had moved before, from a rented apartment to a rented house to "at last our very own home; we'll never have to move again," which, alas, we soon outgrew.

We had bought the home after our fifth child was born, thinking, for some ridiculous reason, that we would not have any more children. Three years and two and a half babies later, we found ourself looking for a new house, which is a chore in itself, but not nearly as difficult as unloading the old house.

Can you imagine trying to "show-and-sell" a home in which seven kids have shared one bathroom, built a tunnel in the basement, scribbled cute sayings on their bedroom walls, and buried God-knows-what in the backyard?

"Don't worry about a thing," the realtor told us when he went through the house. "It's amazing what a little paint and plaster will do."

"And just who is going to apply this paint and plaster?" I asked. "Don't look at me; I'm too pregnant to paint my own fingernails, let alone the kitchen. And don't expect my husband to do it; he can't, 'cause he's a lawyer."

(Note to the reader: Please don't write and tell me that your husband is a lawyer and has just redecorated your whole downstairs. If he wants to get disbarred, that's his business; but I know for a fact that there is some kind of a statute forbidding lawyers to wield paintbrushes, or hang wallpaper, or even carry out the garbage.)

"My brother-in-law knows somebody who dabbles in redecorating," said the realtor (all realtors know "somebody who knows somebody," especially somebodies who can boost the price of a house). "I'll give him a call."

The very next day the "dabbler" dropped by to give us an estimate. He carried his little clipboard from room to room, carefully stepping over toys and toddlers, and made enough notes to cover the reconstruction of Buckingham Palace.

"What do you think?" I asked him when he came back to the kitchen.

"I can get the upstairs painted and the downstairs papered by early March" (this was early December), "but the roof may take a little longer."

"The *roof?*" I exclaimed. "What's wrong with the roof?"

"The color," he said. "We'll replace those shingles with Spanish tiles; they'll blend much better with the brick, which, by the way, really should be tuck-pointed."

"Forget the tuck-pointing," I said, "and forget the roof. All I want is an estimate for the 'little bit of paint and plaster' the realtor said would make this house salable. Can you tell me what that will cost?"

"I'll mail you an estimate," he grumbled, and I later learned why he wanted to mail the bad news. He didn't want to hear my expletives when I learned what "a little bit of paint and plaster" would cost.

"I think we're going to have to forget redecorating," I told my husband. "Maybe we should just advertise the house as a 'handyman's special'?"

"That's the way it was advertised when we bought it," he said, "and since then we've put enough money into this house to rebuild it from the ground up. What happened to it, anyway?"

"We've *lived* in it!" I said. "You can't put seven kids in a house and expect it to stay perfect!"

"No, but I expected it to stay *up!*" he said. "Maybe we can forget the redecorating, but I think we're obligated to replace the back porch. It would be rather difficult to sell a house that has a six-foot step-down out the back door."

So we fixed the back porch, and the front door, and the bathtub faucets, and the furnace fan, but we let the "pretties" go, hoping that prospective buyers would assume we had discounted the price in lieu of redecorating.

As people began to trek through our house, it became obvious that it is not a good idea to "show" a house with kids around. The baby cried every time a strange face peered into her playpen; the four-year-old kept asking questions like: "Why is that fat lady looking in my closet?" and the eight-year-old, who had previously announced that under no circumstances was he going to move out of his home, offered such "helpful" suggestions as: "If you're going down in the basement, watch out for the rats!" Furthermore, we could never show our one-and-only bathroom, because our two-year-old had finally figured out the purpose of the bathroom conveniences and spent most of each day proudly enthroned.

After five or six unsuccessful "shows," the realtor tactfully suggested that for the next "open house" the kids be in absentia.

That's all well and good, but just where does one take seven little kids on a Sunday afternoon in winter? The first Sunday we took them to their Aunt Betsy's. The second Sunday we were going to take them sledding, but it was too cold, so we went back to Aunt Betsy's. After the third Sunday Betsy never seemed to be at home; I wonder where she took all her kids every Sunday that winter? Not to the movies, I know; at least, we never saw her there, and we were certainly there enough.

By Easter we had had exactly one bid on the house, which we gratefully accepted, but unfortunately the deal fell through because of financing. The young couple's parents, after touring the house, refused to cosign the mortgage.

By summer the realtor, who had long since given up being tactful, said, "Maybe if you'd get all this stuff out of here, I could sell this place!"

The "stuff" he referred to was not, as you are thinking, the children. It was our furniture, and believe me, "stuff" was an accurate description.

So we moved out, only to learn later that another couple had decided to bid on the house but changed their minds after they saw it empty.

If you think it is difficult to sell a house that is currently occupied, you should try to sell one that was recently occupied. No matter how carefully you scour and scrub before the movers come, that house is going to look absolutely awful when you go back to lock up after the last load of "stuff" has been carted out of there.

For you would-be home sellers (or buyers, God help you!), here are just a few "eyesores" a homeowner never notices until the furniture is gone:

1. The spot where the refrigerator stood has turned a ghastly green, but you won't notice it unless you scrape up the black guck, which you certainly won't be able to do unless your husband is one of those people who, every third Friday, says: "For cryin' out loud, doesn't anybody ever clean under the refrigerator?" and considerately gets one of the kids to move the refrigerator so you can scrub thereunder.

2. The spot where the sofa was will look infuriatingly new and bright, thus making the rest of the carpeting look filthy. You then have to decide if you should pay somebody $150 to shampoo the carpeting, or just mess up the spot where the sofa was.

3. The walls of your daughter's bedroom are covered with stickum from the tape she used to hang up her posters when you told her she couldn't pound nails into her walls. Learn from this experience: you *cannot* remove stickum; you *can* fill nail holes. (I can't remember what filler you use; according to my son, who spent four years in a college dorm, peanut butter is excellent.)

4. All the window blinds are covered with fingerprints, none of which you noticed when the curtains were hanging. Now you know why so many people sell their curtains along with the house. If you don't intend to leave the curtains, at least remember to roll up the blinds.

5. In the back of the attic, and/or the corner of the basement, there is still a lot of stuff the movers left. Unfortunately, this conglomeration is yours and must be either moved or disposed of. If you choose the latter course, do not share this knowledge with members of your family unless you want to spend the next four years listening to them blame you for throwing out such personal treasures as: a bent basketball hoop, a torn teddy bear, or 412 back issues of *Sports Illustrated.*

A last check of this house your realtor is waiting to show-and-sell will focus your attention on the smoky walls around the heating vents, the fingerprints around the light switches, and the fact that every single faucet in the house has suddenly decided to drip. The filth and grease around the vents and the fingerprints around the switches can easily be washed off, but I wouldn't advise it; you may end up washing the entire house.

As for the drippy faucets, you can either pay a plumber to change all the washers (do not ask your husband to do it, even if he isn't a lawyer; this is no time to put a strain on a marriage already shaken by house-hunting), or you can suggest to the realtor that, as he shows the house, he dash into every bathroom and turn on all the faucets to show "how wonderful the water pressure is!" And it's amazing how wonderful the water pressure is when a house is empty and the shower, dishwasher, and washing machine are not in competition with each other.

Before selling your home, however, you really should take inventory of your young adult children. How many are still living at home? Is anybody planning to move out? Is anybody contemplating a move back home?

I am only suggesting that you *consider* said children, not that you *consult* them. In fact, you should be as secretive as possible about your plans, for if anything discourages an offspring from leaving the nest, or encourages his already-flown sibling to return to the nest, it is the realization that their parents "are making other plans."

Don't say I didn't warn you!

The Lost Generation

As a wife I find his billfold and his glasses,
And I always find his missing comb and key.
I have found the children's books in time for classes;
But now I'm asked to find the missing ME.

They insist my inner being will astound me—
I must tap resources deep within my soul;
And they promise me the moment that I've found me,
There is nothing that could keep me from my goal.

Why does this Women's Movement
Insist I need improvement?
Now I'd go and find myself at any cost
If only I was sure that I was lost!

10

THE LOST GENERATION

"I don't believe this!" I said to my husband as I opened the mail. "I got turned down!"

"For what?" he asked.

"For a bank credit card!" I said. "Remember you told me if I was going to do a lot of traveling as a career woman, I should have my own charge card? Well, I applied for one, and they turned me down!"

"Why?"he asked. "Do they offer any explanation?"

"Yeah," I said, "and wait till you hear it. They said I haven't established any credit. I, who have been paying bills every month for years!"

"But those bills are in my name," said my husband all too logically. "How are they supposed to know who *you* are?"

"How?" I scoffed. "Because I'm the one who signs the checks. I'm also the one who does the charging, and the worrying, and the writing of nasty notes to credit departments who seem to think they should be paid on time. Oh, they know who I am, all right! But you know what is really ridiculous? During all those years when I was overcharging in your name, they didn't say a word! Why, there were some years when I didn't get the Christmas charges paid off till August. Did they complain about that? Of course not! But now that I want a business card that they know will get paid in full every month, they aren't interested! That's discrimination!"

"That's not discrimination, Teresa," he said; "that's red tape. They don't have any way of knowing you intend to use that card for business only; for all they know, you're some swinging single who'll charge up a storm and then disappear. Here, give the letter to me; I'll handle it for you."

"No," I said firmly. "I'll handle it. I just realized why they won't give me a card. I'm nonexistent. I'm not a person; I belong to the lost generation."

The college graduates of the sixties claim that theirs was the lost generation; they spent their years in school, as well as the decade thereafter, trying to "find themselves, to establish an identity," which they evidently succeeded in doing, since they are all now running the country.

Theirs may have been a "mixed-up" generation, but it was not lost. Mine was the generation that got lost.

How did we get lost? We who grew up in the forties and went to college in the fifties never floundered trying to "find ourselves" or "establish our own identities." We knew who we were and where we were, as well as where we were going, when, why, and with whom. How did we know all this? Because somebody—everybody!—told us. Our parents told us where to go to college; our counselors told us what careers we should seek; our employers told us what to do, and our husbands told us everything else. We who grew up serenely content to be daughters, students, wives, and mothers never worried about whether or not we were "individuals" or "persons."

But with the coming of the Women's Movement, all women, even those of us who were content, and even proud, to be Mrs. Somebody, were prodded to become persons in our own right, to express our individuality, to proclaim our independence, perhaps even to establish a career . . . and apply for our own credit cards.

What they didn't tell me was that "being a person" can be exhausting, confusing, and a pain in the neck.

I realized that one morning as I was walking through the Dallas airport, lugging three pieces of luggage (now I know where "luggage" gets its name), holding my airline ticket in my teeth, mentally rehearsing a speech I was scheduled to give that evening, and wondering how I had ever let myself get talked into this. Now, I have been in the Dallas airport many times (nobody has to convince me that its bigger than Manhattan Island; it's bigger than Russia), but I have never been so discombobulated as I was that day, with a briefcase in one hand, an overnighter in the other, a purse slung over one shoulder, and a garment bag weighing down the other. As I struggled toward the check-in counter, an observant airport attendant approached me and asked: "Do you need anything, lady?" and I replied: "Yes. A husband!" For it was not until that moment that I realized that throughout all my travels, my husband had handled all the luggage, held onto the tickets, verified our destination, got us good seats, and sought out the nearest rest rooms.

Incidentally, after hiking through a dozen airports in as many months, I have found the answer to teenage unemployment. Get those kids jobs as skycaps. Sure, there is always somebody in the terminal to take your luggage, but what about the other end of the line? If no friend or relative is meeting you at the gate, you are doomed to drag that "carry-on" luggage two miles to the terminal (where you will then have to tip somebody three dollars to put it into a taxi).

I wouldn't feel so incompetent in an airport if everybody

around me didn't look so competent. (Is everybody in the
country a "person" but me?)

Not long ago I was seated on an airplane next to a petite
young woman who looked like she wasn't strong enough to
carry her purse. Yet when time came for us to deplane, she
pulled a heavy bag out from under the seat in front of her and
hoisted another down from the overhead compartment; then
as she walked to the front of the plane, she deftly removed a
garment bag from the closet, slung it over her shoulder, and
anchored it with the hand that held the briefcase (I don't know
where she put her purse; I think purses must be passé), and
floated right off the airplane as if she were carrying nothing
heavier than a feather. How did she manage it? Simple; she is a
product of the right generation, the sophisticated seventies.
She probably learned luggage-juggling in kindergarten.

I followed her upstairs to the taxi stand and watched, mes-
merized, as she breezed past six well-dressed businessmen,
stepped out into the drive and whistled with all the confidence
of a hotel doorman signaling his favorite cabby. Needless to
say, by the time my turn came, the cabs were all gone. And it
was raining. (It's always raining when us nonpersons are trying to get a taxi.) But I'm learning; after sizing up the situation, I did what any sensible person would do under the circumstances (the circumstances being that I was on an expense
account): I took a limousine. (I felt like I was in a funeral
procession. Where I come from nobody rides in a limousine
unless they have to.)

Can you imagine anybody putting *me* on an expense account? I, who haven't balanced a checkbook in thirty years of
trying; who can't keep track of the cub scout treasury, or even
remember which of my kids is due for an increase in his allow-
ance and which deserves to be dunned?

The first time I was told that I was to be on an expense account, I was ecstatic. I had always dreamed of traveling on somebody else's money, and here was my chance! I would stay in the best hotels, eat in the finest restaurants, and ride around in limousines. It would be terrific!

But it wasn't terrific; it was terrible. I found that when someone has pinched pennies for years and years, it's tough to let go, even of someone else's pennies.

"Why am I staying at the Ritz?" I called my publisher when I found myself ensconced in a plush penthouse suite. (Nobody born during the Depression is at ease in a penthouse suite.)

"Because it's a magnificent hotel, and we want you to be comfortable" was the explanation.

But how could I be comfortable, knowing that my insomnia was costing one hundred dollars a night? I wonder if they would think me gauche if next time I suggested they put me in a midtown motel, and pay me the difference.

Somehow it seemed such a waste, all that space just for me. I should have brought my husband along, I thought, or a couple of the kids—a thought so typical for a woman of my generation. Now a "person" wouldn't think like that; she'd simply enjoy the luxurious accommodations, and probably even consider them her due.

But if I felt guilty sleeping in a suite all by myself, I felt even more guilty walking into that elegant downstairs dining room without an escort. My mother would not approve! (And my grandmother would disown me!) For we girls who grew up in "the lost generation" were taught that "ladies" did not dine out alone. Incredible, but true. It was a theory to which I had never given a thought until I sat in my lonely penthouse suite, contemplating what to do about dinner. A glance at the "room service" menu convinced me it would be much more economical to eat in the dining room, so, feeling somewhat like a wanton woman, I called downstairs and made a reservation for two.

Yes, for two. I was afraid if I admitted that I intended to dine in public, alone, they would call the police and have me arrested.

As the maître d' showed me to my table, I explained that my husband would be along shortly, then spent the next ten minutes glancing at my watch, sighing in disgust, and pretending that I had been stood up.

My guilt in just being there was compounded when I looked at the menu—$37.50 for the Entrée du Jour? Perhaps I ought to order the Entrée du Yesterday; if it was as expensive as today's entrée, it must still be available because surely nobody ordered it yesterday.

"May I recommend the Entrée du Jour?" asked a tuxedoed waiter as he bowed over my table.

"What is the entrée today?" I asked, while still scanning the menu for hamburger.

"Lobster au Beurre," he said, in much the same tone that the serpent must have used when he offered Eve the apple. "The lobster is fresh from the sea."

Fresh lobster! Do you know how seldom a Nebraska seafood lover finds fresh lobster on the menu? But . . . $37.50! My conscience couldn't bear it. On the other hand, my expense account could; and if those who are on expense accounts won't order the lobster, who will? If I don't eat it, it will probably get thrown out. And think how awful that would make the chef feel! All that trouble, to cook fresh lobster, and then nobody will eat it!

The lobster was delicious; so was the shrimp cocktail, the

Chablis, and the chocolate mousse. If I was going to have a guilty conscience, I figured I might as well enjoy it.

But my concern over the cost of my suite and my dinner was minimal compared to my worry over my "out-of-pocket" expenses. In the discussion of my expense account, I had been told to keep track of tips, taxis, etc., so that I could be reimbursed.

Having heard tales of people who "pad" their expense accounts, I determined to be meticulous in detailing every single expense. Thus I had purchased a notebook and pen ("notebook: ninety-nine cents; pen: thirty-nine cents") in order to enter every dime I spent the moment I spent it.

But I found that was not always possible. For example, when I had gotten out of my taxi at the hotel, it had been pouring rain, and as the hotel doorman was waiting patiently to take my luggage (as well as my tip), I didn't take time to write down the taxi fare and tip. By the time I had checked in at the desk, stopped at the gift shop to buy a newspaper and a candy bar, taken the elevator to my room, tipped the bellhop for bringing up my luggage, and the housemaid for bringing me an extra blanket (I miss my electric blanket!), I couldn't remember how much I had paid to whom for what. And if I couldn't remember how much I had spent, how could I get reimbursed?

The solution was simple. That very morning I had cashed a check for one hundred dollars in anticipation of my "out-of-pocket" expenses for this trip. I could just count the money I had left in my billfold, and assume that what was missing should go on my expense account.

However, when I opened my billfold, I found that all I had left in cash was four dollars.

Where had all the money gone?

I mentally backtracked, going over my day from the moment I had cashed the check until the present.

I had driven home from the bank, and as I got out of the car, I seem to remember somebody stopped me in the driveway and asked me for something. Oh yes, he asked for money. (What else?) My son reminded me that his father had threatened to kick him out of the house if he didn't get his hair cut. (I do wish my husband wouldn't force me to make such difficult decisions!) There went twelve dollars.

I had then walked into the house, gone upstairs to get my luggage, when my daughter (who can smell fresh cash) told me she "just had to have" a certain sweater at the teen shop; it was on sale, half-price, "today only" for fourteen dollars.

Then I remember the doorbell ringing—the paper boy. Seven fifty plus tip.

Oh, and I forgot the taxi to the airport! There went eighteen dollars not counting the tip. Then there was the taxi from the airport to the hotel, and the tips—but that still doesn't add up to ninety-six dollars. Where did the rest of the money go? Did I get shortchanged, or could I have dropped a bill somewhere? And if so, who is responsible for it, me or my publisher? Surely, the publisher. After all, I wouldn't be here losing money if they hadn't insisted I make this trip! Now I knew why even the nicest people pad expense accounts!

I have since made many trips on an expense account, and I have learned to make out my expense account just like the pros do. I charge my room and meals to my publisher and submit everything else as "miscellaneous."

I suppose there is a chance that my publisher got charged for somebody's sweater, or even my daily newspaper, but it all works out eventually. After all, I don't bill them when my husband drives me to the airport, and I split the difference whenever he gets a ticket for double-parking.

I am becoming quite sophisticated in this business of "becoming a person," occasionally shedding my role as wife and mother to "find myself" as an individual. I now travel alone without a qualm, carrying one piece of light luggage crammed with wash-and-wear clothes. I've learned how to get aisle seats on airplanes, the room-with-a-view in hotels, a "good" table in restaurants; I've even learned how to hail a cab.

But I knew I had really achieved "personhood" the day I got my major credit card. I felt twenty-one again, carrying my very own charge card, in my very own name, purchasing whatever I pleased, wherever I pleased, without worrying about accounting to anyone! It was great fun!

Until the bill came.

"Honey," I buttered up my husband as we opened our respective mail, "do you suppose you could lend me one hundred dollars till payday?"

"Sure," he said. "Do you want to buy something?"

"No," I said. "I've already bought something. And I've also learned something."

"What's that?" he asked.

"You know how I said I wanted to 'find myself' as a person?"

"Yes," he said.

"Well, I think I prefer being lost!"

Planning the Vacation

My spouse and I are going on vacation.
I've alerted every relative and friend,
For I hope our present neighborly relations
Won't, because of teenage parties, quickly end.
    (The kids are staying alone;
    Aunt Betsy has promised to phone.)

Now the freezer's filled with pizza and burritos,
And I faithfully restocked the pantry shelves
So the children wouldn't fill up on Doritos,
Which would be the menu they would pick themselves.
    And I've written down the number
    Of the electrician and the plumber.

Next, I washed and pressed, and cleaned out all the drawers;
And, in case Aunt Betsy comes to make a check,
I have rid the basement stairway of its horrors,
And I've left behind a house without a speck!
    (Now I need a vacation
    Just from the preparation.)

11

PLANNING THE VACATION

"I need a vacation!" I said.

"Who doesn't?" asked my husband.

"What's a vacation?" asked our daughter.

"I'm not sure I remember exactly," I responded as expected. "But I think it has something to do with getting away from work, the telephone, and, if you'll pardon the inference, children."

"Oh, *that* kind of vacation!" said my husband, brightening. "It sounds like a great idea, but I can't get away just now. Maybe next summer."

"That's what you said last summer," I said, "and the summer before that and the summer before that. That's why I'm suggesting a winter vacation. How about it?"

"I'd love it," he said, "but I really can't get away. Things are hectic at the office right now."

"Things are always hectic at the office," I said. "If you are going to wait for things to quiet down at the office, we might as well forget taking a vacation—ever. There is always going to be something so important and imperative that it can't be done by anybody else. I know you won't believe this, but if you died tomorrow that company would not close down."

"Not even for the funeral?" asked our ultraliteral daughter.

"It wouldn't have to," said our sassy son. "Knowing Dad, he'd deliberately die just before the weekend so the funeral could be on Saturday when nobody would miss work or school."

"An excellent idea," said his father, sarcastically. "I'll keep that in mind when my time comes."

"And that may be sooner than you think!" I said. "I'm serious about this. You need a vacation even more than I do, and I think we should plan one here and now!"

"I have the feeling," said my Beloved, "that you have already planned one there and then."

"Oh, goody," said another daughter. "Where are we going and when?"

"Not *we,* dummy," said her brother, *"they.* Kids don't get vacations! Kids just stay home and wash dishes and scrub floors and carry out the trash and are grateful for a bowl of gruel once a day. . . ."

"Now cut that out!" I said. "I know you kids would like a vacation, too, and I promise you that we'll plan one for you soon."

"Like last year and the year before?" asked another son.

"We didn't get a vacation last year or the year before," said his sister.

"No, but we *planned* one," said her brother. "Mom's great at making plans; she's just not very good at carrying them out."

"And that's all we're doing now . . . planning," said my husband. "Chances are we won't go anyplace. So just forget it and eat your dinner."

I was not about to forget it. It had been years since my husband and I had taken a vacation without our children. That's a typical problem for parents; you can't bear to leave the kids when they are little, and you don't dare to leave them when they are big.

But I truly felt that the time had finally arrived when we could leave our children alone. We no longer had any babies or toddlers who need constant supervision. Our four oldest sons (who, at one point in their lives, I wouldn't leave alone long enough to go to the bathroom) had not only grown up to be mature, responsible adults, but they had also moved out, leaving a fairly manageable size family of only six children. The oldest "at home" was a lovely, capable, reliable daughter of twenty who had the added talent of being sneaky enough to catch our youngest, a lively, rambunctious, carefree boy of twelve, *before* he could get into mischief. As for the four "intermediate" children, I knew I could trust them to stay out of trouble, because while our oldest daughter would be keeping an eye on our youngest son, our youngest son would be keeping an eye on everybody else. In fact, I knew everybody would be supervising everybody else; that's one of the "joys" of a big family: nobody can get away with anything.

So the problem was not so much should we go as where should we go? Contrary to what my son said, I am not very good at making plans, especially when I get little or no cooperation.

"Where would *you* like to go?" I asked my husband when I had given him sufficient time to adjust to the fact that we were going *someplace*. "I was thinking about a cruise."

"A cruise?" he laughed. "You get seasick paddling across the park lagoon! Do you really want to spend a bundle of money just so you can throw up all across the Caribbean? Forget it. Anyway, I don't like cruises."

"How do you know?" I asked. "You've never been on one."

"No," he admitted, "but I've taken enough movie and TV

cruises to know what they are like. You get me on one of those fourteen-days-and fourteen-stops horrors, and *I'll* be the one throwing up all over the Caribbean."

"Do you want to go to the mountains, then?" I asked.

"Why?" he asked. "We don't ski. We don't even après-ski— though after a couple of days in one of those jolly lodges I would probably take to drink. Forget the mountains."

"I've got an idea!" I said. "Let's go to New York! I've always wanted to see the Big Apple! We could take in a few shows, do some shopping, see the sights. . . ."

"Are you out of your mind?" he said. "Nobody goes to New York on purpose! We'd blow our entire budget with one show and one dinner! Why do we have to go anyplace? All we really need is a rest; we can do that right here at home. Why don't I just take off work for a couple of weeks, and we can take in some movies, eat out a couple of nights, just laze around the house. . . ."

"You're the one who's out of your mind, if you think I'll agree to that!" I said. "The last time you took a vacation at home, you spent all your time walking around the house asking how long had it been since I had cleaned this closet or scrubbed that floor. We are going *away!* I'm going to call the travel bureau right now and see if we can get on one of those two-week tours to Europe."

Actually, I had no intention of going to Europe, but I figured if he dwelled on that awhile, my original plan to lure him to Florida would have a greater chance of success.

I had heard about a wonderful resort on the island of Captiva, off the west coast of Florida in the Gulf of Mexico, and I was determined to spend a few days there. I anticipated enjoying the sun and the sea; taking long walks along the beach, eating gourmet meals in those famous restaurants; no doubt about it, this was my kind of vacation!

I made reservations for the following Saturday (a wise wife never gives her husband time to have second thoughts) and immediately plunged into all the preparations necessary for such an extended time away from hearth and home and those who eat and sleep therein.

I bought tons of groceries, and spent one entire day making meatloaves, spaghetti sauce, casseroles, soups, etc.

"What are you doing?" asked my husband when he found me surrounded by food and freezer wrapping.

"I'm stocking the freezer," I said. "I want to be sure the kids have plenty of ready-to-heat-and-eat meals while we're away. You know very well they won't cook for themselves!"

"How can you say that?" he roared. "Every midnight one or the other of our kids is out here cooking something for himself. They make pizza, hamburgers, chili, pancakes; there isn't anything they can't cook!"

How can a man be a father for so many years and still know so little about kids?

"You don't understand," I said. "The same teenager who can whip up a three-course gourmet meal when he isn't supposed to even touch the refrigerator will claim he can't even boil water if it is suggested that perhaps he should feed himself for a few days. That is the law of the land."

"Do these have anything to do with that law of the land?" he asked as he stepped over three overflowing laundry baskets.

"That's right," I said. "I am doing all their laundry even though I know they are experts at doing laundry because I also know that once I am out of the house, if they have any excuse at all for not changing their clothes, they will grab it. I do not want to come to a house where six teenagers have been wear-

ing the same outfits for two weeks. Now, while you are standing there, open that cupboard and hand me the oven cleaner,
will you?"

"The oven cleaner?" he asked incredulously. "Don't tell me
you are going to clean the ovens just for the kids! They
couldn't care less about all that guck in the oven!"

"I am not cleaning the ovens for the kids," I said. "I'm
cleaning them for my mother."

"Your mother? I didn't know your mother was coming. I
thought we agreed that the kids didn't need a sitter."

"She's not coming to take care of the kids," I said. "She
may not come at all. But if our plane goes down, or I should
drown in the Gulf of Mexico, you can bet Mother will be up
here in no time, and she will kill me if she finds out that I died
and left the kitchen looking like this."

"We should have planned this trip a long time ago," he said
as he looked around and saw the newly washed windows, the
freshly waxed floors and the just-replaced refrigerator handle
that has been missing for months.

"You're right," I sighed. "The house is so clean I almost
hate to leave it."

"We don't have to leave it," he suggested hopefully, but I
squashed that in a hurry.

"Forget it," I said. "We're going, and in just two days! I
hope you have everything ready."

"What's to get ready?" he asked. "I'll just throw a few
things into a bag. It's no big deal; you make such a fuss about
traveling."

The next evening I said, "I know our plane doesn't leave till
after noon tomorrow, but don't you think we should start
packing tonight?"

"Good idea," he said, and began to pull clothes out of his closet.

"Did you get those cleaned and pressed?" I asked.

"They don't need to be cleaned," he said. "You can press them for me when you iron my shirts."

"What shirts?" I asked. "I thought I told you to take your shirts to the laundry so they would be folded for packing."

"I was going to," he said, "but I found out they charge ninety cents a shirt! For that, you can do them."

"For that, I would do them," said I, who had often done the whole week's laundry for less than that—much less, in fact. "But when do you think I am going to find time to wash and iron your shirts?"

"You can do it when you wash my pajamas, socks, and underwear," he said. "And if you have a minute, will you choose some ties for me to take? And polish my loafers, will you, when you clean my golf shoes?"

"And just what are you going to be doing that you won't have time to polish your shoes and choose your ties?" I asked.

"Cleaning the basement," he said, and he seemed to be serious!

"You are going to clean the basement?" I asked incredulously. "We are supposed to leave town in less than twenty-four hours; you haven't packed; your clothes aren't even ready to be packed, and you are going to clean the basement? For crying out loud, *why?*"

"Do you think I'm going to let your mother come and find a clean kitchen but a messy basement? It'll only take me a couple of hours. Anything I can do for you while I'm down in the basement?"

"Yes," I said sweetly. "Refrain from watching the Friday

night basketball game on the basement TV." He did not deign to answer.

By staying up past midnight, and getting up five hours later, I somehow managed to get his clothes cleaned, pressed, and packed. I really wouldn't have minded so much, had he not said to me as I was throwing a few last items into my own bag, "Aren't you packed yet? You women! It takes you forever to get ready to go anyplace!"

As we were getting ready to leave for the airport, I remembered!

"Wait a minute!" I said. "We can't leave yet! I forgot to make out the schedule!"

"What schedule?" he asked impatiently.

"The one for the kids!" I said. "If I don't write down exactly what they are to do while we are away, they won't do anything!"

"That could be all for the best," he said, "depending on how you look at it."

I quickly found a piece of paper, and jotted down the following:

Kids: Please read the following schedule and follow it daily:

1. When you get up in the morning, be sure to make your beds, brush your teeth, eat a nourishing breakfast, and clean up the kitchen so you won't come home to a mess.

2. Before you leave for school, turn down the thermostat, check the locks on the windows and doors, and give a key to the next-door neighbor so she can let in anybody who loses their key.

3. Go to school. Go directly to school. Do not stop at the Donut Shoppe. Do not stop at the drugstore. Do not stop anyplace. School starts at eight-ten. Be there.

4. When you come home from school, empty the waste-baskets, clean up your rooms, shovel the walks if it has snowed, do your homework, help your sister get dinner; *do not turn up that thermostat; it is not that cold;* do not turn on the TV unless and until everybody has finished their homework.

5. When you go to bed at night, be sure to turn off the lights, turn down the thermostat (I thought I told you not to turn it up!), put the car away, close the garage doors, lock all the doors, set your alarm clocks, brush your teeth, and say your prayers.

You have our number; call in case of an emergency.

My husband took the schedule, read it over, and said, "Do you mind if I edit this a bit?"

"No, go right ahead," I said, sure that he would add something parental about parties and automobiles and long-distance telephone calls.

He took out his pen, made some changes, and handed it back.

"I think perhaps we should just concentrate on the important things," he said. He had scratched out most of my messages, leaving only the following phrases:

". . . get up in the morning . . . go to school . . . go to bed at night . . . call in case of an emergency."

I was wrong; he knows his kids better than I thought.

On Captiva

All winter I'm plotting and scheming,
Of island vacations I'm dreaming.
From bills overdue,
And from bouts of the flu,
I urgently need some redeeming.

    So we fly to Captiva.

While we sun and we dance and we dine here,   .
We declare that the air's most divine here.
We forget all our fears
About kids and careers.
Oh, we'd gladly retire and decline here!

    We should die on Captiva.

Back at home the debriefing sets in . . .
With the tales of each fault and each sin;
Of suspension from school;
Broken pipes, broken rules;
Our enchantment is changed to chagrin.

    And I cry for Captiva.

12 ⟨⟩

ON CAPTIVA

The island of Captiva (so named because the pirates of old kept lovely ladies captive there) is a present-day haven for middle-aged parents who like to pretend that they are once again young and carefree and attractive and childless.

I knew I was going to love the whole area when we got off the airplane in Fort Myers, Florida, and I didn't see anybody under the age of forty. That city of sunshine is heavily populated with senior citizens, most of whom, after they have been there awhile, begin to think, look, and act, junior. And I soon found out why. No kids. It's amazing how young you can feel when you don't have anybody following you around popping his gum and nagging: "When're we gonna eat?"

"Okay, this is your trip," said my husband as we walked through the terminal. "Where do we go from here?"

He knew very well where we were going, but he was rubbing it in. I had insisted on making all the plans for this trip. (Otherwise, I knew he would have booked us into a hometown motel for a weekend, with a second-night cancellation clause.) It was quite an experience for me, as I had never, ever planned a trip. In the twenty-six years we had been married, my husband had always taken care of the details of our trips. (Both of them.) Consequently, I had never made an airline reservation, typed an itinerary, booked a hotel room, checked luggage, rented a car, or tipped a bellhop. I had no idea there was so much to be done, but I enjoyed making all the plans, reservations, and arrangements.

Unfortunately, however, I got off on the wrong foot. Or more specifically, the wrong flight.

"Is there any particular reason," my husband had asked when we were checking in our luggage prior to takeoff, "why we are taking a midnight flight to Florida? Don't they have any daytime flights?"

"Oh, sure," I said. "They have lots of them. But this was the cheapest! We got the night rate!"

"I hope we also got a direct flight," he said. "I am in no mood to play hopscotch all the way to the Gulf of Mexico."

Of course we did exactly that, because I had forgotten to inquire about direct flights and had cheerfully accepted the first "economy package" she suggested. I had also cheerfully responded: "Oh, I will!" when she had said: "Standby?" Fortunately, there are plenty of seats on the Midnight Special, so we did get a seat, though I had forgotten to specify "Smoking" and my husband had a nicotine fit from St. Louis to Atlanta.

"Okay, we're here," my husband said when we finally arrived in Fort Myers. "What now? We'll never get a taxi at this ungodly hour."

"We don't need a taxi," I said, "I rented us a car. It's all ready and waiting for us; we can pick up the keys over there at the rent-a-car counter."

"You mean the one that's closed?" he asked, and sure enough, there was a sign on the counter saying: WE OPEN AT 6:00 A.M.

"So what if we have to wait a bit!" I said. "That will give us time to get breakfast in the coffee shop . . . just as soon as it opens."

Actually, it was just as well that we did not get the car until daylight. (True, it's not daylight at 6 A.M. But it was daylight by the time we had signed the rent-a-car forms, presented our credentials, argued about price, agreed on insurance coverage, and found the car in that crowded parking lot.) I would have been devastated had we driven to Captiva in the dark and missed the gorgeous scenery, or worse, missed that sharp turn and driven into the Gulf of Mexico.

To get from Fort Myers to Captiva, one must first drive across the causeway to Sanibel Island, in itself famous for its fabulous resorts, unique restaurants, and beautiful beaches. As we drove up Sanibel, I began to wonder if I had chosen the wrong island; surely Captiva could not be more beautiful than this!

But it is! After we drove across a shorter causeway that joined Sanibel to Captiva, I began to fall under the spell of that tropical island so loved by Anne Morrow Lindbergh, who made Captiva famous through her book *Gift from the Sea*. The sea had never seemed so blue, the sand so white; the trees so lush, and green, and gorgeous.

It wasn't until we drove into the fabulous resort on the north end of Captiva that I got up the courage to tell my husband that I had reserved not just a hotel room, but a condominium—not for a weekend but for a whole week.

"You've committed us to an expensive condominium for a *week!*" he said. "We'll go bankrupt! And we'll go crazy! I don't want to hang around this place for seven days! What will we do for a week?"

He felt a little better about the expense when he realized that the kitchen in the condominium would mean we could limit our meals in the superb gourmet restaurants, and he felt better about the isolation when he realized that he could keep in contact with the office by telephone—and that I was not going to force him to swim in one of the many pools, or play tennis on one of their professional courts, or even deep-sea fish in the waters of the Gulf.

"I just want to walk on the beach," I told him, "and sleep late in the mornings, and read one whole book without interruption! I promise this will be a quiet, tension-free week."

And it would have been, too, if it hadn't been for the telephone. (Notes for next vacation: Find a place without a telephone.)

He spent the whole first day on the telephone, talking to various people at the office, frustratingly trying to carry on business as usual from a thousand miles away.

By the second day I had convinced him that the office could run without him, and lured him out on the beach—at least till sundown. Then it was back to the telephone.

"Who are you calling now?" I asked, when he brought that hateful telephone out onto our moonlit porch overlooking the Gulf.

"The kids," he said.

"What kids?" I asked dreamily, as I sipped my Kahlúa, listened to the surf, and counted the stars. (It doesn't take me long to forget.)

"*Our* kids!" he said. "Don't you think we'd better check up on them?"

"Why?" I asked. "We've only been gone two days. What could have happened to them in two days?"

"I'm not worried about them," he lied. (Why is it that an at-home father can go for weeks without asking about his kids, but get him away for a couple of days and he imagines them in all kinds of terrible predicaments.) "I just don't want them worrying about *us.*" (Ha! That'll be the day.)

"Call if you insist," I said, "but I think it's a mistake."

"Why?" he asked. "We'll talk only a minute; it won't cost much."

"Oh, no?" I scoffed. "Remember the time we called home just to tell the kids where I had left the car keys, and you talked for twenty-five minutes?"

"That was different," he said. "The kids were all little then; naturally they wanted to talk to us. They're teenagers now; they won't want to 'waste' more than a minute talking to us; they never do!"

He had forgotten that unwritten rule of the adolescent: Never talk to your parents unless it's going to cost them at least seventy-five cents a minute; then talk their ear off.

"Darn it," he said, "I forgot my credit card; I'll have to call collect."

He placed the call, and in a few moments our son Patrick answered, and I heard the operator ask him if he would accept a collect call from his father.

"Nope!" said Patrick, cheerfully.

"Patrick!" yelled his father. "Take this call!"

But the operator had already disconnected the call, informing my husband coldly that our party would not accept the charges.

"Why would Patrick do a thing like that?" asked my husband, furious.

"Because you told him to!" I said. "Don't you remember when John and Mike kept calling collect from college, and Jim kept reversing the charges from overseas, you told the kids never to accept a collect call from *anybody,* not even God?"

"That didn't include *me!*" he said. "Now what are we going to do?"

"Simple," I said. "Wait till Patrick has gone to bed, then call again and one of the older kids will answer."

So we did. At eleven o'clock that night I called home, and got no answer!

"Something's happened!" I cried. "It's midnight there. Why doesn't anybody answer?"

"Maybe they're all asleep," said my husband. "After all, it's almost twelve o'clock."

"Yes," I admitted, "but it's twelve o'clock midnight, not noon; why would they be asleep?"

"Wait a few minutes and try again," suggested my husband, and I did. In fact, I called every five minutes for the next half hour, but still we got no answer. I was frantic. Where was everybody? There were supposed to be seven kids there; surely they all couldn't be out? Maybe there had been a fire and they were all outside? Or worse, all *inside!*

"What are we going to do?" I wailed.

"Forget it," said my husband. *(Now* he wants to forget them!) "We'll try again in the morning."

But I knew I'd never make it till morning. I finally called our next-door neighbor, got him out of bed, and persuaded him to go over to my house and check on our children.

A few minutes later, our phone rang.

"Hi, Mom," said our daughter Mary. "Were you trying to call us?"

"I've been trying to call you all evening!" I said. "Where have you been?"

"Right here," she said. "Where else?"

"But why didn't you answer the phone?" I cried. "Don't tell me it was unplugged!"

"Nope," she said, "it's been working fine. Are you sure you dialed the right number?"

"Of course I dialed the right number!" I said.

"Are you sure, Mom?" she asked. "What number did you dial?"

"*Our* number!" I said. "556-8019!"

"Mom," said Mary patiently, "our number hasn't been 556-8019 since 1975. Don't you remember, we got a new number when we moved."

Well how was I to know? I haven't been anyplace since 1975; why would I have had any occasion to call home?

It took about three days on Captiva before my husband could be convinced that both the office staff and our kids could survive without constant telephone communication. After the third day, I didn't even have to hide the phone anymore. Of course, I did have to cut the plug off the television set (never take a winter vacation with a football freak), but once we got that out of the way, the week was marvelous.

We walked on the beach, searching for seashells, watching the sea gulls and sandpipers, listening to the sounds of the surf, leaving our footprints in the sand and our hearts on Captiva.

We fell in love with Captiva and fell in love with each other, all over again. Like everyone who goes to that magical island, we shed our worries and our years and became young again—and attractive and carefree and romantic and childless!

We came home to a typical Nebraska blizzard; it took almost as long to drive from the airport to home, creeping over ice-coated streets, as it had taken to fly the last leg of our trip. When we finally pulled into our driveway, we saw the light in the window (in every window, it seemed) and the kids on the doorstep. We were home!

"Hi, Mom and Dad! What did you bring us? I need four dollars for the seventh-grade field trip—"

"Annie broke your blender making milkshakes—"

"Guess what? Peg got a speeding ticket and gets to go to court—"

"Jim drove Dad's car while you were gone and I told him you would kill him; will ya?"

We were home, all right. Boy, were we home.

Strictly Personal

There are letters from friends
And letters from foes,
Letters that comfort
Or add to my woes,
Letters of cures which my savings would take
Or from entrepreneurs
Who would sell me a lake;
If I'd like to be cold
And undriably damp,
Would I like to be sold
A Saskatchewan camp?
Letters which come
With their postage collect;
Then there are some
Which I must redirect.
But the letters of which
I'm increasingly fond
Are those I can ditch
Since I needn't respond.

13 ⌒⌒⌒

STRICTLY PERSONAL

When the book *Strictly Personal and Confidential: Letters Harry Truman Never Mailed* was published, a zillion people ran out to buy the book to see if they were in it, or to see who *was* in it and to read what old Harry had to say that was so bad he had second thoughts about mailing the letters but so good he couldn't bring himself to destroy them.

I bought the book because I was sure it would include a letter to me. I had written to President Truman to express my thoughts about his sending American troops to Korea when I was currently being courted by a first lieutenant (and who did the President suggest I take to the Mardi Gras Ball?). Alas, the President did not deign to answer my letter, either mailed or unmailed, which can only mean that Harry's reply remained in his mind, along with the very best of all his correspondence.

For while the letters we never mail are better than those we do, the letters we don't write at all are the cream of our correspondence.

I myself have written dozens of letters which, for one reason or another, never got mailed. (One reason being I gave the letter to one of my kids to mail; another being my spouse said I'd get sued.)

But my very best letters are those which never see paper, let alone postage: letters to teachers, notes to neighbors, epistles to my pastor, fan letters, fun letters, letters of reference requested by persons who worked for me (or more literally, did *not* work for me). Some people vent their spleen on the psychiatrist's couch, others at the dining room table. I vent mine at the kitchen sink, where I compose scathing letters while scouring pots and pans.

Often these imaginary epistles are composed either before or after I have written the actual letter, and some go way back to my childhood, such as the note my mother made me write to a neighbor whom I had allegedly "assaulted." The letter I really wrote read:

> Dear Mr. S:
> I am sorry that I kicked you in the leg yesterday when you told me not to walk on your grass. Please accept my apology.

The letter I would have liked to write would have read:

> Dear Mudface:
> Remember yesterday when you yelled at me just 'cause I knocked my croquet ball into your yard, and when I ran to get it I tripped and kicked you in the leg? I wish now I'd kicked you in the nose!

Then there was the note my mother made me write when I won the high school composition prize. It read:

> Dear Reverend Mother:
> Thank you for the beautiful plaque; I shall treasure it always.

When it should have read:

Dear Reverend Mother:

The plaque is okay, but if you really want to make points with the kids, make the prize a Frank Sinatra poster.

Other letters I have written, first actually and later mentally, include the following:

Dear Mrs. G:

Thank you for the unique clock you sent us for a wedding present. We shall place it on our mantel, and think fond thoughts of you every time we look at it.

Though if I had been totally honest, I would have written:

Dear Mrs. G:

Thanks for the kooky-looking clock. Since we couldn't figure out where to take it back, we are going to put it on our mantel and laugh like crazy every time we look at it.

And:

Dear Mother and Dad:

Guess what? I am expecting again. Isn't that great? Lee is so thrilled! The baby will be a first birthday present for Michael, and I know little Lee and John will be excited to have another sibling, even though they are just three and two years old. It will certainly be fun to have four babies under four!

Surely my parents read the words between the lines:

Dear Mother and Dad:

You guessed it; I'm pregnant again. Aagghhh! Lee says the same.

My notes to teachers are the phoniest of all. Like the following:

Dear Third Grade Teacher:

My sincere apologies for my son's behavior during study hall yesterday. Of course he should not have spent his study time writing all those notes to the girls in his class. I appreciate your sending the notes home, and we have punished our son accordingly.

My husband said I should have written:

Dear Teacher:

Hey, how about this kid? Pretty clever, huh? He can not only write, but what a sense of humor! Thanks for sending the notes home; we have put them in our scrapbook.

And:

Dear Junior High Principal:

My son tells me that there was a scuffle in the seventh grade classroom for which he was partly responsible, and he will not be allowed back in class unless he brings a note from his parents indicating that disciplinary action has been taken. Be assured this has been done.

Though I am tempted to write, and someday probably will write:

Dear Principal:

My son tells me that he needs a note. This is a note.

What I really hate writing are letters of reference for people who have worked for me but not very competently, like the kid who used to take care of our lawn—sort of. When he applied for a job with a lawn service, I wrote the following letter for him:

To Whom It May Concern:
    John is a fine, hardworking boy who will take on any task you give him and do it cheerfully.

I only hope his would-be employers can read between the lines:

To Whom It May Concern:
    John is a fine, hardworking boy who has a tendency to goof off frequently, but he will take on any task you give him and do it about as competently as a three-year-old, however cheerfully.

Some of my letters never get written at all, but this does not preclude me from composing them mentally for my own gratification. Like fan letters. I have never had the courage to write a fan letter, but I have composed several, if only in my mind. Like the following:

Dear Paul Newman:
    After careful consideration I have concluded that I would rather run away with you than with Robert Redford. Just name the day! I'm sorry it can't be Tuesday, I have cub scouts that day. And Wednesdays are out because I have car pool. Thursdays are tricky, too, unless you want to meet me in the grade school cafeteria (I'm Assistant Clean-up), and Fridays my teenagers take my car. I'm sure you will understand that my weekends are spoken for, but how about Monday? (If you can't make it, would you pass this on to Robert Redford, please?)

And:

Dear President Nixon:

I don't care what anybody says, I think you are a good guy. But I do have one question about the Watergate tapes: Couldn't you find any matches?

Or:

Dear Captain Kangaroo:

Don't you *dare* retire! True, I wrote you some years ago that my children are all in school and I didn't need you anymore, but now I have a grandchild. I *need* you!

Then there are necessary notes which I truly wish I had the time to write, such as:

Dear Chairman of the Nominating Committee:

I know what you are thinking, and the answer is NO.

And:

Dear Mr. Friendly Banker:

If you're so friendly, why do you keep sending me nasty notes? I got your notice of my overdrawn account; you didn't have to follow it up with that mean letter. Here is your money, plus the penalty. How could the penalty be more than the amount of the overdraft?

And:

Dear Father Pastor:

I see on the eighth grade acolyte schedule that my son is scheduled to serve 6:30 A.M. mass every day through February. Forget it, Father. It's noon mass or nothing. This is my seventh acolyte, and I am much too old for dawn patrol.

And then, of course, there is the Christmas letter we all dream of writing one day:

Dear Family and Friends:
Happy Holidays! I know you have been eagerly awaiting my annual newsletter. It's been quite a year at our house, what with our daughter Gilinda's divorce dragging on and on, but she is free at last! (Or she will be as soon as her husband moves out. I am beginning to regret ever letting them live here.)

Gilinda's sister, Granada, canceled her wedding plans again. That girl! She's as changeable as the weather. She says to thank you all for the gifts, which she has carefully stored with the ones you sent last year.

Sonny writes that reform school isn't as bad as he expected, now that he has found some friends who share his interests. (Frankly I didn't know they allowed that sort of thing in reform school, but I am not about to complain. They might send Sonny home.)

Who said hobbies can't be turned into jobs? We are so proud of our son Eldred, who has been a photography buff since grade school days. He has spent the last year in Washington, where he has a lucrative career selling negatives to politicians.

If any of you see Little Al (we must stop calling him "Little Al," after all he is almost thirty years old!) would you please ask him to call his mama? He jumped bail again, that naughty boy!

I hope you all have a Happy New Year!

It may be filled with lies, but at least the relatives would read it.

Unfortunately my own Christmas letters are dreadfully dull, as nobody ever does anything very spectacular at our house. In fact, I was seriously considering forgoing this year's holiday letter, but my mother insisted that I write one, at least to her.

"But Mother," I argued, "there is never any news!"

To which she replied: "I know, dear, but you must understand. To a grandma of young adult children, no news is good news!"

The Misery Makers

The misery makers among us
We meet every day of the week;
Those various villains who've stung us
With rudeness or boredom or cheek.

The first on my list are the preachers
Whose sermons detain us too long.
And students complain that their teachers
Are never just where they belong.

Who stealeth my good cleaning lady
Should get five to ten for the theft.
And parking spot nabbers are shady
To leave me of space so bereft.

The fellow who's dialed the wrong number
Reacts as though I'm in the wrong.
In motels, I'm roused from my slumber
By revelers shouting "So long!"

The driver who's crowding my tailgate
While honking with gesture so rude,
I'd love to see ent'ring a jail gate
For manners and methods so crude.

Those bullies of childhood, when grown up,
Berate all the waiters and clerks.
As children they should have been blown up
Before they grew into such JERKS!

You all know some misery makers,
Who probably act even worse.
So Friends, I'll accept any takers
To write me an end to this verse.

14

THE MISERY MAKERS

While some people, either inadvertently or advertently, make life more enjoyable, others, all too often advertently, make our lives miserable. I am not referring here to obvious "meanies" such as terrorists, teachers, and prospective mothers-in-law (the latter two I admit I once was or still am, and the former I am sometimes tempted to be) but rather the otherwise pleasant person who, when placed in a particular environment or faced with a specific circumstance, turns into a real saphead.

For example, consider the Wrong Number Caller.

There are two kinds of Wrong Number Callers: male and female. However, it is not the female Wrong Number Caller who "makes misery." When she realizes that she has misdialed, she says, "Oh, I'm so sorry; forgive me for disturbing you." It is the male Wrong Number Caller who, when he dials a wrong number, either hangs up without a word (thus leaving the wrong number fearing that she's the victim of some crazy —and she is) or he says: "Who is this? I couldn't have dialed the wrong number. You must be in the wrong house!" I don't know why the male Wrong Number Caller can't bring himself to admit that he has misdialed; with these teeny-tiny push buttons, an occasional error is certainly forgivable.

What is not forgivable is the Repeat. The Wrong Number Repeater is the fellow who, having dialed a wrong number, immediately redials the same number without first checking the telephone book, because he is confident that he could not have been at fault; the "telephone company must be goofing off again." Thus the wrong number has to get up and answer the telephone again, only to have it slammed in her ear because if there is anything a Wrong Number Caller hates more than getting a wrong number, it's getting a wrong number twice in a row.

There are so many "misery makers" in this world I cannot possibly list them all, but I have chosen a "favored" few, rating them in the following manner:

* People who are only occasionally frustrating and can probably be *forgiven*.

** Characters who are frequently frustrating and should be *forced to take an est course*.

*** Jerks who are so consistently unbearable they should be *run out of town*.

**** Goons. *Eliminate them*.

The Theater Talker. Oh, for the good old days, when theatergoers spoke only in whispers, and not at all during the performance! There is nothing so disconcerting as trying to hear dialogue over and above the constant chattering of someone seated near you. I admit that their conversation may be more fascinating than the show itself (in which case you may want to turn around and say: "Either speak up or shut up!"), but the fact remains, they are making everybody's evening miserable and deserve ***.

The Car Pool Tard. (Well, what do *you* call someone who is tardy?) In this energy-saving era, many office workers car-pool to work, and inevitably, there is one member of the pool who is never ready when you honk in the morning and always delayed when you are ready to leave at night. This Tard gets **. (Unless he is the son-you-gave-a-job-to-because-he-wouldn't-look-for-one-elsewhere, in which case you may want to consider ***.)

The Never-There Professor. Where *do* profs disappear to between classes? Most faculty members have offices (or at least cubicles) with specific office hours posted, but my college kids claim that the "prof is never there." A pox on the professor who assigns a complicated term paper or project, says, "If you have any questions, see me after class," then walks out the door into oblivion. Sorry, Prof, you get **.

The Engine Revver. Anyone who has ever been awakened at midnight by someone revving an engine, either auto or motorcycle (why can't he "idle" it gently? Why must he make it go THURRRDDADDLA . . . THURRRDDADDLA . . . THURDDADDLA . . . ?), will understand why the Engine Revver is rated here with **. (I'd like to give him ***, or better yet ****, but he's dating my daughter and I'm trying to be tolerant. See paragraph one, this chapter.)

The Manic Driver. All of us cautious, prudent, law-abiding drivers resent the driver who tailgates us, honking wildly, waving angrily, and sometimes even yelling at us just because we aren't going fast enough or slow enough to suit him. Without hesitation I give that maniac ***. (And if he adds an obscene gesture, he gets ****.)

The Forty-five-minute Homilist. Priests and ministers sometimes wonder why babies who are sleeping soundly when the church service begins burst into loud wails about the middle of the sermon. There is a reason for this. Babies are the only parishioners courageous enough to complain when the sermon is too long. **(For the homilist, not the babies.)

The Casual Caller. Nobody enjoys visitors more than I do; I even welcome the "surprise" caller who drops in unannounced. But the person who "drops by for just a few minutes" and stays for hours is an annoyance and deserves **. (Unless she brings goodies, in which case she rates only *.)

The Parking Space Grabber. There should be a particular punishment meted out to the driver who zooms into the parking space for which you have been patiently waiting and for which you were obviously headed. May a UPS truck drive up and block him for hours! ***

The Bully. Whether it be the "big kid" in grade school who picks on the "wimp," the "big mouth" in high school who taunts classmates and teachers, or the supposedly mature adult who castigates clerks and grabs on-sale outfits right out of another customer's hands before I even had a chance to try them on, the Bully of any age rates ****.

The Popcorn Eater. I am not referring just to those people who noisily chomp popcorn in a movie theater (***), I also mean anybody at all who eats popcorn, with the possible exception of the person who can eat popcorn without spilling any, if there is such a person, which I doubt. Anybody who has ever had to clean up after a popcorn eater knows why the P.E. is listed here with either * or **, depending on how often he eats popcorn. If its caramel corn, its definitely **.

The Cleaning Lady Thief. Nobody likes a cleaning lady who steals (***!—though if she does windows, you might change that to *), but by Cleaning Lady Thief I don't mean a cleaning lady who steals; I mean a person who steals cleaning ladies. If you are one of the homemakers fortunate enough to have a terrific cleaning lady, for heaven's sake don't tell anybody or by next Thursday you will be outbid for her services. The Cleaning Lady Thief definitely deserves ****. (I know **** is harsh, but with *** she's liable to take the cleaning lady with her, and ** is too lenient. Cleaning lady thieves never change their ways; they just keep looking for better cleaning ladies.)

The Reformer. I certainly commend anyone who can diet and really lose weight, who can stop smoking and not gain weight, or who can run ten miles a day and feel terrific, but if she doesn't shut up about it she's gonna get ****! (even if she *is* my sister).

The Show-Off Driver. I don't care how pleasant and polite he is when he's not behind the wheel of a car, the fellow who sped down our street and deliberately drove across my front lawn (if it wasn't deliberate, why was he shouting "Wheee!") will, if I ever catch him, get ***!

The Irresolute Job Interviewer. While I appreciate how difficult it must be for a job interviewer to tell an applicant that he doesn't pass muster and might as well look elsewhere, there should be a law requiring him to do so. Either a phone call or a postcard would be appreciated by the guy waiting to hear if he got the job (and even more appreciated by his mother who's tired of hearing him say: "But I can't go out and look for another job; Slaves-For-Hire may call me"). To the job interviewer who says, "We'll call you," and doesn't: **.

The "Over-There" Dog Owner. As a former dog owner who spent a decade dutifully following her Irish Setter around with a pooper-scooper, I know what a nuisance it can be, but dog owners who let their pets out for their morning "constitutional" and send them "over there" to the neighbor's yard should certainly get **. (And if they send them over *here,* it'll be ***!)

The Underestimator. When will auto mechanics, house painters, paperhangers, and the like learn that we would rather have them bid the job at three hundred dollars and then charge two hundred fifty than we would have them bid two hundred fifty and then charge three hundred? The most popular mechanic in our town tacks twenty-five dollars onto each job bid, then, when the job is done, announces cheerfully, "I was able to save you twenty-five dollars!" The Underestimator, sadly, deserves his **.

The Hotel-Motel Reveler. Why is it that people who tiptoe and whisper in their own homes if others are sleeping, will clatter, chatter, and sometimes even yell in a hotel corridor at three o'clock in the morning? Surely such thoughtlessness deserves **. (And if I'm sleeping in that hotel, anticipating an appearance on an early morning television show, it may well be ****.)

Who's Who

It is not What but Who I know,
The experts all agree,
Will bring my name to early fame;
But do they guarantee
That Mr., Mrs., or Ms. Who
Admits to knowing me?

15 ⎯⎯⎯⎯⎯⎯

WHO'S WHO

"It's not What you know, but Who you know" say the cynics, and I'll have to go along with that, but one What everybody should know is Why we must cultivate the Who's.

For example, a child in grade school, just learning his What's, would be well advised to make friends with the smartest kid in the class so that they can share ideas, as well as answers. For failing such a friendship, the child will have no recourse but to be nice to his teacher, or worse, settle down and study.

High school students don't have to be told why it is expedient to get on good terms with such Who's as the hall monitors, the school newspaper reporters, or the woman who dishes out desserts in the cafeteria, but how many sophomores realize that the most important Who in their high school career is the school secretary, for she is the one who sets the course the kids will follow the rest of their lives. (You can drag your feet through four years of classes, back-talk the teachers, and ignore the principal's calls to the carpet, but if you place one rose on the secretary's desk you'll be referred to forever as "an exceptional student.")

College kids are well aware that the only Who they need to know is the campus computer, for in every college or university, it's the computer "who" sets the schedules, tabulates the grades, credits the accounts, and sends letters to parents advising of academic probation and disciplinary action.

However, once we leave school and enter the big, complicated world, the Who's we need to know become too numerous to list, let alone explain. Aside from the obvious ones (the president of the company for which you'd like to go to work, or a compassionate clerk in the employment agency) there are at least ten Who's you really must become friendly with in order to survive. These include:

A plumber. There is only one thing worse than coming down to the kitchen on a weekday morning, when you have to go to work or plan to be out all day, and find your kitchen sink stopped up, and that is coming downstairs on a holiday morning, when fourteen relatives are coming for lunch, and find your kitchen sink stopped up. The "good old days," when you could call a plumber and before you had hung up the phone and scooped the floating garbage out of the sink he'd be there, are long gone. Nowadays the plumber may be there, but you won't; you'll either be at work, or at a committee meeting, or perhaps car-pooling the kids. It is a good idea, therefore, for you to make friends with a plumber who will come before nine or after five or at least at a time when you can arrange to be home. When you go searching for such a plumber, try to find one who is also in the furnace business, because if there is anything more frustrating than having your sink stop up on the Fourth of July, it's having your heat go off on New Year's Eve.

A mechanic. Anyone who has ever come out of the office at five o'clock and dashed through a heavy rainstorm to the haven of his or her car, only to discover that the darn thing won't start, will understand why it is important to develop a relationship with a mechanic. Unless you are the type of person who can repair whatever's wrong with a couple of paper clips and a rubber band (and if you are such a person, you undoubtedly have paper clips and rubber bands readily available in the glove compartment), you really must get to know a good mechanic. By "good" I do not necessarily mean someone exceptionally talented in the care and maintenance of automobiles (frankly, anybody who can keep the darn car rolling will do); I mean somebody who is so *good* that when you call him at five o'clock in the midst of a heavy rainstorm he'll *come*. (Today.)

A tailor and/or seamstress. (Why aren't they called tailoress and seamster?) Unless you are a five-foot-six, one-hundred-ten-pound female (or a five-ten, one-hundred-eighty-pound male), the clothes you buy won't fit, not the day you buy them and certainly not next year when you have put on ten or fifteen pounds. Blessed be the alterations person who can turn an on-sale size eight into an on-me size ten, but even more blessed be the tailor who can not only make my husband's suits fit (both before and after the annual diet) but can also "erase" the occasional burn from a carelessly flicked cigarette ash. (You don't really appreciate a tailor until your husband burns a hole in his Ultrasuede sportcoat, though you appreciate a seamstress the first time you try to hem a pleated skirt. I don't care how good you are at the sewing machine; pay somebody to hem your pleated skirts.)

A barber and/or a cosmetologist. Nothing makes a man grouchier than the need for a haircut, and if you can't con a barber into fitting old Shag into an already overbooked day, it could be a long, hairy (in more ways than one) weekend. Since the sexes are now equal, I must admit that a woman in need of a shampoo-and-set can be every bit as antsy as her shaggy spouse, especially if an "event d'importance" is scheduled for Wednesday night and her "standing" at the beauty shop is on Thursday. So cultivate a barber-cosmetologist who will care enough about you to "fit you in."

An insurance agent. Only after your first automobile accident will you appreciate the "need to know" your insurance agent. So what if the accident occurs at two o'clock in the morning? Your good buddy won't care if you wake him up to ask him what your liability is, and he certainly won't have the heart to remind you, at that ungodly hour, of your two-hundred-fifty-dollar deductible. Furthermore, if you get to be very, very friendly with your insurance agent, you won't feel so bad when you tell him: "Heck no, I don't want to double my life policy; I'm already worth more dead than alive."

A good used-car salesman. I have never understood why used-car salesmen are listed so far down on the popularity polls. Personally, I have never met a used-car salesman who wasn't charming, cheerful, and exceedingly friendly, though my husband claims that "it is their business to be charming, cheerful, and exceedingly friendly; just contact one three days after you bought the car when the transmission falls out and see how friendly he is." But that is precisely why I advocate making friends with a good used-car salesman. I don't mean the salesman must be good; he can be rotten to the core for all I care, as long as he sells me a good used car.

A travel agent. Who needs a travel agent, you ask? You say you can make your own reservations? Fine; go ahead and make them. But who are you going to blame when the airline overbooks, the hotel loses your reservation, the rental car breaks down, or your luggage gets lost? Many a marriage has been saved by a caring travel agent who good-naturedly took the blame for a lousy vacation.

A lawyer. You may never need one, but make friends with one anyway, if only to have a name you can throw out when-and-if you ever have to threaten to "call my lawyer" and your adversary asks, "What's his name?" Having a "family lawyer" is every bit as important as having a "family doctor," especially if you have a family who tends to forget such things as tax estimates, traffic rules, and building codes. (Personally, I don't see how such a teeny-tiny tree house could be illegal, do you?)

The editor of the local newspaper. The editor of your local newspaper is an important person to know for several reasons, the main ones being (1) he can use his influence (and he probably will) to get a news item into the paper for you, and (2) he can use his influence (though he probably won't) to keep a news item out of the paper for you. In any event, newspaper editors are fascinating people to have as friends, not only because they know "all the news that's fit to print" but also because they know all the news that isn't!

A cleaning lady. In this era when almost all women have careers, the most important Who you may ever need to know is the woman whose career is domestic service: the "cleaning lady" who comes once a week to shovel out your living room, counsel your kids, and generally put your house in order. When both husband and wife are working outside the home, a competent, reliable cleaning lady is a joy to have, a friend-in-both-need-and-deed, the ultimate Who. And if you want to know the reasons why, come to my house any day but Thursday.

Leave It to Pepys

Mr. Pepys would have his say
In his gossipy old way,
His stories losing nothing in the telling.
Of the famous he told tales,
Sending readers into gales
But did you ever see such awful spelling?

Of King Charlie and his Nell
Very naughtily he'd tell,
Though scandal of this kind so seldom keeps.
If they fought with phrase or fist,
And when reconciled, they kissed,
Old London heard it first from Mr. Pepys.

Were Mr. Pepys alive today,
Residing in our U.S.A.
Our peccadillos he would no doubt gather.
More than likely he would be
Telling all on NBC
The very time I'm listening to Rather.

(The English swallow half their words,
So said some learned Preppys,
That's why they call him Mr. Peeps,
And never Mr. Peppys.
But he was both, if you ask me,
According to his diary.)

16

LEAVE IT TO PEPYS

For Christmas my eldest daughter gave me a handsome leather-bound, gold-embossed book—with blank pages.

"This should be a quick read," I quipped, "and it's my kind of book: no long descriptive passages, no gory violence, no explicit sex. It leaves a lot to the imagination. I can't wait to read it."

"This book isn't for reading, Mother," my daughter explained patiently. "It's for writing. It's a journal. Our psychology professor said that everybody should keep a journal. By writing down the events of the day and expressing your innermost thoughts and feelings, you will develop a greater understanding and appreciation of life."

"I already appreciate life," I said, "probably because I don't understand it. This is a lovely gift, and I know you put a great deal of time and thought into choosing it, but I don't think I can bring myself to write in it."

"Why not?" she asked. "It's a convenient size, has quality paper, a beautiful binding . . ."

"That's the problem," I said. "It's too beautiful to write in. I was brought up to believe one *never* wrote in a bound book.

Couldn't you have given me a spiral notebook or three-ring binder instead?"

"Don't be silly, Mother. This book is for posterity, like Pepys's diary. You are a writer, lecturer, and author; you may be famous someday! You should record your life for those who come after you!"

I wished she hadn't mentioned Pepys. His diary is the most famous journal of all time. Written over three hundred years ago, it is still considered a classic. How could I compete with that?

I couldn't, of course, but I concluded that keeping a journal might be fun. I wouldn't try to make it a daily diary; I'd just jot down events and ideas as the mood hit. If I didn't produce a journal for posterity, I would at least have something to entertain my grandchildren. I certainly wouldn't let this journal become a chore or complicate my life.

Before I had written one word, that journal became a chore and complicated my life.

There is more to keeping a journal than keeping a journal. First you must decide whether to make your entries in pencil or in pen. Do you want to be able to erase, edit, or even delete? Do you really want this thing to be *permanent?* If so, should you use blue or black ink? Fine, medium, or broad point? Felt-tip, fountain, ballpoint, or rolling ball? Decisions, decisions!

You must decide when would be the best time to write in your journal. Early in the morning? Late at night? Surely not during the day. Anybody who has anything interesting to write in a journal doesn't have time to write during the day.

Then you must decide where to keep your journal: on your desk, for anyone and everyone to pick up and read? In your bureau drawer, hidden under your nightgowns, where only your children will come across it? In your attaché case, where it will be lost among your unfinished projects and unpaid bills?

I opted for pencil (I change my mind a lot), late at night (the only time there is quiet), and my bedside table, which presented another problem. Where, on my already over-crowded bedside table, would I find room for a journal?

I don't need a journal to "portray my true self"; my bedside table tells more about me than anybody should ever know. True, it's a bit messy, but everything on there is necessary. There is a reading lamp (with two ways of the three-way bulb burned out; who can bring themselves to discard a light bulb that still works, even if it is only thirty watts?), a book or two (or maybe three in case I finish one or get bored with another), an alarm clock, a box of nose tissues, a flashlight (anybody who lives in tornado territory sleeps with a flashlight), a notepad and pencil for writing reminders to myself (if some-body would just remind me to read them), and the sweetest, most endearing picture of one of our babies (though I can't remember which one, which is all right; that makes it sort of an all-purpose picture).

After taking inventory of everything on my bedside table, and weighing the priorities, I did the only thing feasible: I bought a bigger table.

At last I was ready to begin my journal.

December 28: This morning I went to the dentist; he told me I needed a root canal, and since his next appointment had canceled, he could do it then and there. I do not intend to "record for posterity" my "innermost thoughts and feel-ings" about a root canal. I didn't feel much like going on to the Guild Luncheon, but as secretary I felt I should be there. I forgot I had to read the minutes. Never attempt to read minutes when you have a faceful of Novocain. Nora

Murphy insisted on helping me back to my table; Patty Monahan moved we no longer serve wine with our luncheons, and Alice Gump leaned over and whispered to me that she "knows somebody in A.A." (I'm not surprised.)

January 3. I went to the doctor today for my annual checkup. He told me to quit drinking and smoking. I told him I neither drink nor smoke. He then suggested that maybe I should go on a diet. I then suggested that maybe I should go home, take up drinking and smoking, and come back in a month and start all over again. Why don't doctors ever suggest that mothers take a vacation? Or even a nap?

January 4. Went shopping today for a new living room sofa. Gads, what prices! Who makes those sofas anyway—Rumpelstiltskin? When I was single, I furnished a three-room apartment for what I paid for this sofa. Yes, I bought it; I justified the expense by not buying the matching chair.

January 6: Sofa delivered today; looks lovely! Rest of living room looks lousy. I suggested to my husband that we get new carpeting; he said absolutely not. New drapes? No! I know! Matching chair! He deigned not to answer. That must mean yes.

January 8: New chair delivered today, and it doesn't match sofa! Whatever made me think it did? Can't return either as both were on sale. Maybe if I squint when I sit in the living room I won't notice.

January 12: Hosted dinner party for the Nerdniks and the Glockenspiels. Dick Nerdnik got drunk and spilled brandy all over the new sofa; Gladys Glockenspiel got tipsy and spilled brandy all over the new chair. Now they match. (The sofa and chair, that is, not Dick and Gladys, unless what I heard at the Club is true, which I doubt.)

January 13: Wrecked my car today; some idiot in a Cadillac got in my way! Called police; police ticketed wrong idiot. Called lawyer; he laughed and said: "Wait'll your kids hear about this!" Called insurance agent; he laughed and said: "You have a two-hundred-fifty-dollar deductible; that tin can you drove was worth two hundred seventy-five dollars. Congratulations! We'll send you a check for twenty-five dollars." I have to appear in court. I haven't been to traffic court since the older boys were teenage terrors. I wonder if it'll be the same judge.

January 20: It was the same judge. He said, "Hi, Teresa" and I said, "Hi, Sam" and he said, "Who's the offender this time?" and I said, "I am" and he laughed and said, "Ten dollars and costs!" I'm glad everybody thinks this is so funny; personally, I am not amused.

January 24: Another Sunday. I swear they come twice a week.

4:30 A.M. Got up and drove our son-the-paperboy around while he delivered those "too-heavy-to-carry" Sunday newspapers;

5:45 A.M. Drove our son-the-acolyte to church to serve early Mass;

6:00 A.M. Drove our daughter-the-candystriper to hospital for early shift;

6:20 A.M. Picked up acolyte at church;

6:30 A.M. Cooked breakfast for acolyte and paperboy;

7:00 A.M. Loaded dishwasher and cleaned up kitchen;

7:20 A.M. Drove paperboy to deliver "lost" newspaper;

7:30 A.M. Cooked breakfast for husband and self;

8:30 A.M. Loaded dishwasher and cleaned up kitchen;

9:00 A.M. Made beds, scooped dirty clothes off son's bedroom floor and tossed them into washing machine; helped son search for shoes;

9:10 A.M. Rushed to laundry room to investigate loud noise; removed son's shoes from washer, mopped up laundry room, lectured son, ignored rebuttal;

10:00 A.M. Cooked breakfast for late risers;

10:30 A.M. Loaded dishwasher and cleaned up kitchen;

11:00 A.M. Went to church; subject of sermon: "Sunday, Our Day of Rest"; stifled hysterics;

Sunday P.M. Somewhat of a blur; I seem to remember cooking, loading the dishwasher and cleaning up the kitchen, but that may have been earlier, or later, or last week.

January 27: Monthly meeting of the Housewives' Hobbies and Recreation Club. President Sandy Smith called the meeting to order and took roll. All members were present except Millie Mertz, Cindy Hagar, and Margaret O'Hamski. Linda spoke up and said Millie hadn't been at afternoon bridge club and maybe she was sick. Sally said that was certainly possible as everybody knows how Millie's been hitting the bottle ever since her husband hired that sexy secretary who can't even type. Sandy asked if anybody knew where Cindy was and Shirley said it being Wednesday Cindy was probably still at the Club where she sometimes stays late to play a round with golf pro. I said I didn't know Cindy played golf and Shirley said who said anything about golf. Carol said she didn't think Margaret would show up, as her neighbor Emily had told her that somebody said

Margaret had to go to Chicago for her Aunt Lucy's funeral. Vera said this is the third time since Thanksgiving that Margaret had gone to Chicago; Eunice said this is the third time Margaret has gone to her Aunt Lucy's funeral and didn't anybody think it was odd that Margaret's lawyer always went along. New member Nora Niles interrupted to ask what hobbies and recreations our club advocates, and Sandy said that was a good question; we'd take it up at the next meeting assuming everybody showed up. Nora said she couldn't speak for anybody else, but she certainly intended to show up.

February 1. Carson called again; insists I be on *Tonight.* I told him I couldn't make it; try Joan Rivers. Joanne Woodward called to ask if Paul was here and I told her of course not, don't be silly. (He'd already left.) The editor of *The New York Times* wrote to apologize for omitting my book from the best-seller list but, as he explained, there are only ten places and Bill Buckley needs the ego boost. (Coincidentally, Buckley called later; wanted to ask me the meaning of a word.) Betsy Bloomingdale wrote to ask if it was okay if she told her pal Nancy Reagan that we are related even though we're not and I said sure, go ahead. Sandra O'Connor called to ask my opinion of a case, but I couldn't talk to her as I had Steven Spielberg on the other line; he wanted to discuss the movie script for my book. I told him I haven't decided whether to go movie or Broadway musical, as Merrick suggested. I'll think it over while we're vacationing in the Bahamas.

My daughter read my journal the other day and chastised me for "making up" that February 1 entry.

"You're missing the whole point, Mother," she said. "This

journal is supposed to be an account of your life, a portrait of you to pass on to your grandchildren, maybe even to posterity. Anybody who reads this will think you are a kook. Now please, try to be more accurate. Remember Pepys!"

I do remember Pepys, and the thing I remember best about Pepys is the fact that he was a terrible bore.

Frankly, I'd rather be remembered as a kook.

Plastic Sacks and Other Mistakes

People with headaches are constantly copin'
With aspirin bottles reluctant to open.
Vegetable shoppers, in looking for sacking,
Can find only sacks with the opening lacking.
If, using plastic wrap, you unreel it,
Remember, you know, that you never can seal it.

I find application of each new invention
Shortchanges somehow its creator's intention.
Staplers and lawn mowers can leave you despairing,
For neither is used without first some repairing.
Why must the postage stamp glue taste so icky?
And why are my envelope flaps never sticky?

Things that use batteries drive to distraction;
Just when I need them, they go out of action!
Young children cry when their toys start to sputter;
Flashlights that fade can make anyone mutter.
But the goof guaranteed to make modern man vi'lent
Is when the computer goes suddenly silent!

17

PLASTIC SACKS
AND OTHER MISTAKES

According to the experts, we will someday be able to switch on our television sets and do all of our grocery shopping by remote control. As we push buttons to indicate our choice of canned goods, meats, fresh produce or fine wines, an electronically controlled robot will push a basket up and down a supermarket aisle, responding to our instructions to pick up six pork chops or a pound of ("Pinch those first to be sure they're fresh!") peaches. The robot will freezer-wrap the meat, put the produce into plastic bags, box up the bakery goods, and have your order ready for pick-up or maybe even home delivery.

I don't believe it. Oh, I believe it's possible to produce such a marvel, and I have no doubt that consumers will welcome it and supermarkets cooperate with it, but I'll tell you who won't go for it, and that's the robots.

Robots may work willingly in the beginning; after all, it's something new and it sure beats the heck out of stoking a furnace at the smelting plant, but eventually they will rebel. Any robot who is sophisticated enough to recognize a ripe peach isn't going to put up with the frustration of trying to open those plastic bags one is expected to put the peaches in. You know the ones I mean: those on-a-roller, tear-here sacks that, in the unlikely event you can get them off the roller, never seem to have an opening. You can rub, peel, slip, slide, rip, tear, curse, and swear, but it will do no good; that plastic bag is sealed on all four sides. Unless he's missing a few nuts and bolts, no robot is going to put up with those plastic bags at the produce counter—if he even makes it to the produce counter. He won't last through the first aisle if he gets one of those wobbly, stubborn shopping carts.

Personally, I think the country's inventors should put those robots on "hold" until some of the previous inventions are either shaped up or eliminated. For example:

Plastic wrap. Like plastic bags, plastic wrap is great in theory but impossible in practice. As its inventors predicted, it will cling to anything, especially more plastic wrap. In fact, you can barely pull it away from itself. You can be gentle or firm, tender or tough; it will fight you all the way. I once watched the filming of a television commercial in which a homemaker was supposed to plastic-wrap a bowl of fruit salad in preparation for a picnic. By the time the director was able to say "Cut and print," they had used up four bowls of fruit salad, three rolls of plastic wrap, and six homemakers. (Two quit; two broke down and had to be tranquilized; one just wandered off the set never to be seen again, and the successful sixth was nominated for an Emmy.)

Plastic . . . period. As a mother, I have long advocated the abolition of plastic toys (all of which will break at the whim of a toddler, though I'd be the first to admit a toddler's whim can be brutal), but it wasn't until my telephone melted that I turned truly antiplastic. It seems the whole world has turned into plastic—plastic dishes, plastic furniture, plastic clothes. We don't need a nuclear reactor to cause a melt-down; one hot summer day could do it. I hate to admit that I am old enough to remember such things, but I long for fine china, solid wood, genuine leather, real silk! Expensive? Have you priced Ultrasuede lately?

Talking computers. While I appreciate all the remarkable things that computers can do, I think we will rue the day we taught them how to talk. I mean, it's one thing to have a computer in your car telling you to "BUCKLE UP!" or even one in your refrigerator reminding you that "YOU'VE ALREADY HAD LUNCH: NO SNACKS!" But where will it end? Do we really want our oven to shout: "CLEAN ME! CLEAN ME!" our clothes to cry: "I'M WRINKLED; PRESS ME!" or our car to plead: "I'M OLD; REPLACE ME"? I should hope not. Computers are like kids; they are a wonderful addition to any household, as long as they SHUT UP.

Bottles with safety caps. Like plastic bags at the produce counter, bottles with safety caps really have no openings. The so-called cap is in reality part of the bottle itself, and can only be removed by an electric saw, a monkey wrench, or a two-year-old boy. However, I appreciate the necessity for safety measures, and respectfully suggest that all you inventors who are working on such things as robots concentrate instead on something that could be a real challenge: a toddler-proof cabinet lock.

Teeny-tiny push buttons. Who is the idiot who decided that "smaller is better"? When push-button telephones were invented, I, ever impatient with the rotary dial, was delighted—until the buttons were minimized to such a size I can barely see them, let alone punch them singly. Even worse than miniphones are "pocket calculators," now so small they'd get lost in a toddler's pocket (and often do). No wonder we have inflation; if economists are using those teeny-tiny calculators, they could double-digit us into infinity.

Carbon paper. Despite the fact that we now have photostat machines, duplicators, word processors, and electronic typewriters, many executives still want carbon copies, which means that many typists are still doomed to dirty fingers. (Though perhaps it's too late; I haven't used carbon paper in years, and my right index finger is still Midnight Blue.)

Staplers. Staplers were invented, I am sure, for the sanctification of secretaries. It has been estimated by experts that a secretary spends one fourth of each day either fixing a "sprung" stapler, looking for the correct-size staples, refilling the empty stapler (no matter how frequently she fills it, it will be empty when she wants to staple something), prying out staples that "went in bent," or removing "went-in-straight" staples because the boss wants to change a word on page four. Viva la paper clip!

Bugs. I realize that God created all living things, but I think somebody slipped bugs in when He wasn't looking. I'm not talking about insects—cute little ants that my grandson loves to lie in the grass and watch, caterpillars that turn into beautiful butterflies, glowworms that light up a summer night. I'm talking about *bugs,* those yucky things that crawl out from under rocks, or worse, from under bathroom cabinets. Ugh! (I'm not surprised it rhymes with bug.)

Forms. From birth certificate to death certificate, we live out our life in forms. Immunization records, dental records, school registrations, report cards, health forms, permission slips, applications for driver's license, insurance forms, job applications, diplomas, college applications, marriage licenses, tax forms—it never ends. How did people live in the days when there were no forms to be filled out? Or were there always forms to be filled out? Have archeologists discovered cavemen carvings that read: "Give name, address, zip code, area code, phone number, and social security number; print clearly; DO NOT WRITE IN THIS SPACE"? I wouldn't doubt it.

Dirty ashtrays. There are few things more disgusting in life than a used ashtray, but in formulating the suggestion that we do away with such I realized that would be futile; the stale, smelly things would just be replaced by clean ashtrays that would soon get dirty. Therefore, I suggest we do away with *all* ashtrays, thereby forcing smokers to catch the ashes in the palm of their hand. After a few burns, maybe they'll quit smoking, and make the whole world healthier.

Offensive commercials. I am not referring only to the obvious offenders: ads for laxatives, deodorants, and feminine hygiene products. I am also referring to those commercials which insult my intelligence as well as my sensitivities. If I ruled the networks, I would ban all commercials about upset stomachs, stuffy noses, flaky dandruff, pounding headaches, and any itch anywhere. I would do away with dancing underwear, talking margarine, bouncing bathroom tissue, and people who clutch an empty bread-spread jar to their bosom as they frantically dash through a midnight rainstorm—clad in bathrobe and slippers—to buy more. And I would forever eradicate endorsements from athletes who use atrocious grammar, housewives who appear with curlers in their hair, teenagers who pop their gum while talking, and anybody-at-all who is in the midst of taking a shower. Frankly, the only commercials I can stand are those featuring Catherine Deneuve, Ricardo Montalban, Bill Cosby, and Mikey. (And though I have never been a beer drinker, I might be tempted to imbibe if they would bring back those cute little bears "from the land of the sky-blue water.")

Price tags on picture frames. The world's worst sadist has to be the fellow who invented the price stickers that are stuck on picture frames, and when I say "stuck," I mean *stuck.* Despite helpful hints from Heloise, Mary Ellen, and my mother, those picture-frame price stickers cannot be removed—not by scraping, not by dissolving, not even by destruction; I once dropped a picture frame and the entire glass shattered, except for the corner with the price sticker. Perhaps frame manufacturers could be persuaded to at least put the sticker in the same corner each time, thus photographers could pose a picture with that sticker as part of the scenery.

Postage stamp glue. The world's second worst sadist is the guy who concocted the glue used on postage stamps. With a zillion "flavors" in the world, why did he have to pick "Yaagghh"? What's the matter with chocolate? Coconut? Cognac? With a little ingenuity (maraschino cherry?) they could put the U.S. Postal Service back in the black.

Marriage and the Reader's Digest

Who *is Carolyn Davis?*
Were I to go to Pleasantville
I'm sure my most exciting thrill
Would be to meet
And stop and greet
Carolyn.

Do you suppose she really is?
Has anybody seen the phiz
Of Carolyn?

I wish my friends and family
Would write me half as faithfully
As Carolyn!

18 ∽

MARRIAGE AND THE *READER'S DIGEST*

My husband and I can never get a divorce, because while we might readily agree on who should get the custody of the kids (Grandma), and who should pick up the payments on the car (the kids), we would never be able to reach a compromise on an equitable division of our accumulated "wealth." I am not referring to stocks, bonds, or certificates of deposit (when you have ten children—or *any* children—you do not accumulate stocks, bonds, or certificates of deposit). I am referring to that "wealth" which you do accumulate when you have children (and probably even when you don't)—a treasury that fills our living room bookshelves, overflows into the dining room, the family room, and the front hall, and can even be found upstairs, reposing under our children's beds. Our wealth? A multitude of products purchased over the years from *Reader's Digest.*

This is all my mother's doing. When my husband and I got married, my mother gave us a subscription to *Reader's Digest,* I suspect for two reasons: (1) she felt that no family is complete without one, and (2) she wanted to be sure we didn't borrow hers.

In that latter theory, she was only safeguarding the security of her own marriage. In my father's house, the *Reader's Digest* was sacrosanct. It was my father's favorite magazine, and while we children were all allowed to read it, we were also expected to return it promptly and with pages intact, unwrinkled, uncornered, and unstained. God help anybody who took it out of the house, or borrowed it and neglected to return it, or worse, borrowed it and *lost* it.

I could understand my mother's concern about *Reader's Digest.* But I did not realize that she had a third motive in giving us that subscription: she wanted to be sure that we would stay married forever, as couples must if they accumulate a *Reader's Digest* collection.

I wouldn't want you to think that our house is inundated with old magazines (though I must admit, I find it difficult to throw away old issues of *Reader's Digest;* I am so certain that *someday* I will take time to sit down and figure out those Quiz Features). No, when I refer to our *Reader's Digest* collection, I mean more than the magazine. As anyone who has ever subscribed to *Reader's Digest* knows, there is more to subscribing to *Reader's Digest* than just subscribing to *Reader's Digest!* If just mailing in an annual check for that little monthly magazine were all that's involved, anybody could get a divorce. It's what comes after that gets you hooked—the tempting brochures offering *Reader's Digest* Condensed Books, the nostalgic notices about the *Reader's Digest* Records and Tapes, the intriguing letters describing the *Reader's Digest* Special Editions, and the *real* clincher: the exciting entries in the *Reader's Digest* Sweepstakes.

Our problem is: when it comes to *Reader's Digest* (or I should say "when it comes *from Reader's Digest"*) neither my husband nor I can say no. We love their magazine; we are avid collectors of their books, and we are addicted to their splendid stereo recordings. However, it is not just the current magazine, or this quarter's book, or next quarter's record album that enthralls us; it is anything at all, no matter how dated, that was ever produced in Pleasantville.

My husband and I have spent many Saturdays scrounging through stacks of books in secondhand bookstores or at neighborhood garage sales seeking volumes of the *Reader's Digest* books that were published "before our time" (that is, before we became members) or to fill the gaps created when we inadvertently lost books. Many of those gaps were made by a tornado that took our home and almost everything in it in the spring of 1975. At that time, a pleading letter to Pleasantville brought a wonderful response; the personnel at *Reader's Digest* were most helpful in attempting to replace books we had lost, as well as tapes and record albums that had been destroyed (though they did stop short of asking Frank Sinatra to rerecord "That Old Black Magic" just for me).

Thanks to *Reader's Digest* and secondhand book dealers we were able to restore most of our *Reader's Digest* collection. However, in filling the gaps in our *Reader's Digest* collection of condensed books, tapes, and records, we have added other *Reader's Digest* products which we somehow missed in earlier mailings: mystery books, maps, paintings, sculptures, etc.

Thus, the Bloomingdale household now has a basement bulging with magazines, a living room lined with books, a family room filled with recordings, and a front hall whose floor-to-ceiling cabinets are stuffed with miscellaneous educational or entertaining material produced in Pleasantville. This does not include the *Reader's Digest* products that are periodically stacked on our dining room table, or the teenage books and records that can be found amidst the clutter of our children's bedrooms.

One cannot walk through our home without seeing someone reading, listening to, playing with, working on, quoting from, puzzling over, looking at, or searching for something from *Reader's Digest.*

In spite of the superabundance of wealth that we have acquired from *Reader's Digest,* I suppose a competent divorce lawyer could, if he put his mind to it, divide said wealth equitably between two parties—or, if one must include our offspring, twelve parties.

What he could not do is figure out which party should be the rightful owner of the subscription, and if you think that is not important, then you have never haunted your mailbox hoping to find a *Reader's Digest* notice that you have just won the $100,000 Sweepstakes.

My husband would claim that since he is the one who pays for the *Reader's Digest,* he should inherit the wealth, but I would counterclaim that paying is the easy part; it's corresponding with them that counts, and while it is true that he sends in the magazine subscription each year, along with the check, I am the one who must then keep track of all future transactions, including subscriptions to their other products, changes of address, queries, recriminations, cancellations, explanations, apologies, reconciliations, resubscriptions, and here-we-go-again.

The confusion that frequently results from my correspondence with *Reader's Digest* is not, I must admit, the fault of the people in Pleasantville, or even of their computer (which is invariably, and infuriatingly, correct!). No, the fault is mine, or to be more accurate, my husband's, for he is the one who keeps changing our name. Well, he doesn't actually change our name; what he changes is the name on our *Reader's Digest* subscription.

He does this for one simple reason: to get the gift discount. When you have ten kids, you have to take advantage of every discount offered, and one of the advantages of having ten kids is the fact that you have ten names to feed into the *Reader's Digest* computer, thus giving you an entire decade of discounts.

However, changing names every year causes that computer to go into a frenzy of correspondence, some asking Former Subscriber why it has canceled and some offering New Subscriber the multitude of *Reader's Digest* products.

As that computer is noted for its perseverance, its correspondence with former subscribers may continue indefinitely; thus almost everyone in our family is now receiving mail from *Reader's Digest,* and I am never too sure which one is the active account. If I inadvertently pay an inactive account, the computer launches an intensive effort to reinstate the active account (which, now in arrears, is assumed to be inactive) while at the same time increasing its correspondence with the inactive account (which, having been inadvertently paid, is now assumed to be active).

This confusion is compounded by the fact that the *Reader's Digest* computer is not yet old enough to call subscribers by their first names. Thus their mail to us is addressed to "A. Bloomingdale" or "P. Bloomingdale" or "J. Bloomingdale" or "M. Bloomingdale," and we never know if they mean Arthur or Ann, Patrick or Peg, Jim or John, Mike, Mary, or Margaret, not to mention Mr. or Mrs. (and in the event the letter was announcing a sweepstake winner, you can be sure we wouldn't be mentioned).

Actually, "Mr." or "Mrs." couldn't be included, because my husband never renews the *Reader's Digest* subscription in either his or my name. He won't put it in his name because then he can't take the gift-subscription discount, and he dare not put it in my name because he doesn't want to run the risk of making me "independently wealthy" with my very own *Reader's Digest* collection. He knows very well that as long as we are bound together by our *Reader's Digest* subscription, we can never contemplate divorce.

So you can understand my panic when I opened our mailbox yesterday and found our recently renewed *Reader's Digest* magazine (whose computer has evidently come of age; it's now using first names), addressed to "Teresa Bloomingdale." Worse, it was addressed to *"Miss* Teresa Bloomingdale." Was my husband trying to tell me something? Or is that computer just trying to get revenge for all the extra work I have imposed on it over the years?

I couldn't take a chance. I immediately wrote to *Reader's Digest* and canceled the subscription in my name. In a separate envelope (how else could I get the gift discount?) I renewed the subscription in my husband's name.

I have no fear that he will take his *Reader's Digest* subscription and run, for while I know how much he will love having his very own *Reader's Digest,* I also know that now he will have to keep me around forever, just to keep up with all the correspondence from that computer!

The Lost Convertible

My ancient station wagon has expired.
The engine missed; the gaskets all were dripping.
I know the shocks and springs had all retired
And neither brakes nor tires did any gripping.
                                        It was past reviving.

It weathered well the endless errand chores,
And carting kids to Little League and scouting.
It drove to schools and pools and countless stores
But crumbled more with each successive outing—
                                        And teenagers' driving.

Its last trip out, the poor thing hit a tree.
The only thing to do was pay the towing.
My next car's going to be for only me.
Those kids will have to walk to where they're going!
                                        That's called surviving.

19 ❧

THE LOST CONVERTIBLE

"I've got bad news for you, ma'am," the insurance adjuster said when he called me from the auto repair shop. "Your station wagon has had it; it's finished; kaput. The whole front end is gone. If you hadn't been driving such a big, heavy car you might have been killed. I'm surprised you weren't hurt; that sure must have been some tree you drove into!"

"I did not drive into a tree," I said. "I slid into it. Or rather, my station wagon slid into it. Are you sure it can't be fixed? It's practically brand-new!"

"Brand-new?" he asked. "Are we talking about the same vehicle? The wagon they towed in here has to be six or seven years old."

"It's eight, actually," I admitted, "but that's only on the outside. Everything inside is new. In the past eighteen months I have replaced the tires, the battery, the muffler, the alternator, and starter, and both the front and rear brakes. And just last week they rebuilt the transmission. I haven't even paid for that yet! I intended to drive that car another three years! Surely if they can get new parts for the inside of an automobile, they can get new parts for the outside!"

"They said they'd try, ma'am," he said, "but don't count on it. I handle a lot of these cases, and it's almost impossible to find parts for a car this old. If I were you, I'd start shopping for a new car."

I hate to admit this, but I have never before gone shopping for a new car. Oh, I have tagged along with my husband when *he* went shopping for a new car, but I never paid much attention because I was too busy pouting. Every time we buy a new car, it's for *him*. He claims that he has to drive the new car because of some nonsense about depreciation and tax deductions. I told him I could depreciate a car just as efficiently as he can, and he said that while he wouldn't question that, the IRS might. So while he gets the new car, I fall heir to his hand-me-down, which by now has depreciated to the point where it is ready to fall apart. Inevitably, three weeks after I start to drive the thing, the muffler will fall off, or the brakes will give out, or the starter won't start, none of which would bother me so much if he just wouldn't say, "I swear I don't know what you do to cars; this one was in perfect shape when I gave it to you!"

While I would regret losing my investments in that station wagon, I must admit that I would not mourn the passing of the wagon itself. There is a time and a place for a station wagon, and my time, if not my place, has passed. (Well, almost. It's true we still have four teenagers, but as they are the tail-end of ten, we consider them to be almost adults.) In any event, I am no longer at an age where I have to cart around car seats and play pens, kindergarteners and cub scouts, cheerleaders or soccer teams, or even groceries-for-twelve. After two decades of car-pooling, I am more than ready to trade in that washable vinyl for plush velour!

But alas, I wouldn't be trading it; my husband would trade it for a new car and I would inherit his. Or would I? Somehow I couldn't see my husband giving up the car he had purchased for himself the last time we needed a car. At that time he, too, anticipated the end of our station wagon era and, to celebrate his promotion, had treated himself to a Cadillac. He was crazy about that car, and I doubted that he would consider "handing it down."

"You don't want that great big Cadillac!" he said. "As short as you are, you'd be lost in it. I suppose we will have to get you a new car, but you don't want anything like a Cadillac; you should really think small."

"All right," I agreed, "how about a small Mercedes? Or a petite Porsche? Or a little-bitty Bentley?"

"How about a little bitty Chevy?" he suggested. "Or a pint-size Plymouth? You really don't need anything very fancy."

Who said anything about *need?* Whatever happened to *want?*

What I wanted, whether I needed it or not, was a convertible. I have always wanted a convertible, ever since I was in college, but all I have ever driven are coupes, sedans, and station wagons. I was tired of suitable, sensible cars; I wanted a convertible!

A woman should never take her husband along when she goes to buy herself a car. I took mine along because I felt I had to; I needed him to interpret the window stickers. You know the ones I mean; the long sheet glued to the window of new automobiles that list the equipment, accessories, and price. I have never been able to decode those lists, and for good reason. The abbreviated technical terms don't make any sense, and for that matter, neither does the price. I really think the customer should be told that the list price covers only things like wire-wheel covers and rear-window defoggers. If you want such "accessories" as an engine, seats, or a steering wheel, they're extra. Also, that list price is only for customers who are prepared to pay cash; those of us who have to finance the car should multiply the list price by about four.

However helpful my husband might have been with the window stickers, taking him along was a mistake. He didn't want to look at convertibles; he wanted to look at family-style sedans, and the salesman immediately led us to that area. While my spouse and the salesman discussed such dumb things as safety features and fuel consumption, I tried in vain to ask about important items, such as a stereo radio and color-coordinated upholstery. I had told both my husband and the salesman that I wanted a colorful car, perhaps something in Caribbean blue, or Emerald Isle green. They suggested I should stay with washed-out white or blah black.

Of the three of us, one of us shouldn't have been there, and I think it was me.

Or maybe it was the salesman. I realize that in order to buy a car one must deal with a salesman, but by the same token, if one wants to sell a car, he should deal with the person who is buying the car—in this case, me. I hate to say this, gentlemen, but I do believe that car dealerships are the last bastion of male chauvinism. Automobile salesmen are not yet ready to accept the woman buyer.

In an effort to shape up the system, therefore, I offer here a few suggestions to car salesmen everywhere:

When a husband and wife walk into your showroom, greet the wife every bit as effusively as you do the husband. True, he may be the one paying for the car, but she is the one who talked him into buying a new car, dragged him to your showroom, and will nag him until he makes a decision. You can rattle off technical terms all afternoon to the husband, but you are wasting your breath if you don't take time to sweet-talk the wife, because before any husband will sign a new-car contract, he is going to turn to his wife and say: "What do you think, honey?" If Honey has been ignored, you're in trouble.

If a man walks into your showroom and he's alone, ignore him. He is "just looking." He may buy, but it won't be today. There isn't a man alive who can bring himself to spend that kind of money without the moral support of either a wife, girl friend, best friend, or boss. On the other hand, if a woman walks into your showroom and she's alone, hop to it; she's there to buy. Since women got liberated they are much too busy to browse.

Whether you are selling to a couple or an individual, lead them first to the most expensive car on the floor. They may not buy it, but they'll certainly be flattered that you "assumed they would want the very best." The exception here would be a couple accompanied by their children. Such a couple obviously cannot afford an expensive car (however much they may want it), and they won't thank you for making it necessary for them to spend the next six months explaining to their kids why some parents prefer meals to Mark VIs.

It is not only the salesmen who need shaping up. Automobile manufacturers also are at fault. Perhaps the salesmen could sell more cars if the cars were better equipped. I don't know who designs cars, but I am convinced it is somebody who doesn't drive or even ride in cars. I base this assumption on the fact that most cars are missing some very important equipment.

For example, a compass. Have you ever seen a car with a compass? I have seen cars with computers, telephones, television sets, even a typewriter, but I have yet to see a car with a compass, and I can't imagine a more important piece of equipment. Who of us has never been on a busy highway, frantically struggling with a road map while our spouse shouts: "Are you sure we're going east? We'd better not be going west because there's not another off-ramp for ninety miles! Look at that map and tell me if we're going east!" Think of how many marriages could be saved if cars had built-in compasses!

Another left-out accessory is a litter bag. The only autos I have seen with built-in litter bags are the superexpensive luxury cars. Isn't that silly? People who drive luxury cars don't have litter. People who have children have litter. There should be a litter bag in every family car; several in station wagons.

Another accessory that seems to be reserved for the luxury car is the "keyless entry system," a push-button combination lock which makes it impossible for a thief to steal your car even if he should get hold of the key. This, too, is ridiculous. Rich people don't worry about having their car stolen; that's what they carry all that insurance for. It's parents of teenage drivers who worry about having their car stolen, as insurance companies are slow to pay stolen-car claims made by the father of the thief.

Cars should be divided into categories, with a separate sticker list for each category. If auto manufacturers showed a little originality with accessories, they'd sell a lot more cars.

For example, if a car had:

———————A built-in water fountain;

———————A wet-towel dispenser;

———————A built-in toy compartment;

———————Star Wars seat belts;

———————A front seat back low enough for a parent to reach over and swat;

———————Single seats, with each seat having its own window;

——————Washable seats, walls, roof, floor, doors, handles, etc.
just think how many would sell to families with small children!

On the other hand, a car featuring:

——————A built-in refrigerator;

——————A built-in bottle opener;

——————A stereo radio that automatically returns to rock station after parent has used car;

——————A telephone with message-recorder and call-forwarding;

——————Cable television with video recorder;
would certainly placate those teenagers whose parents refused to buy a Mark VI, and if it also has:

——————A luminous clock that bongs curfew;

——————A stain-resistant, spot-resistant, scuff-resistant interior;

——————A computer recording that announces, when the ignition is turned off: "Lights off? Got your keys? Picked up your Burger Basket remains? Got your sweater (comb, brush, makeup, jacket, gym shoes)? Are you home? If so, come in. If not, then WHY ARE YOU PARKED?"
would probably appeal to the parents, as well.

A more sophisticated version of the above might also have:

——————Reclining seats (note: no bucket seats);

——————Police radar warning system;

——————A built-in bar;

——————A quadraphonic stereo system;

——————A coded computer readout reminding driver of "which one is in the passenger seat tonight";

—————————A simulated "Engine trouble; pull over and park!" light.

It would surely sell like hotcakes to swinging singles.

For the business and professional person, today's luxury cars offer anything and everything anyone could possibly want, from elegant interiors to power-everything.

But what of *my* category? What should a car offer the woman-who-spent-twenty-years-toting-kids-and-now-deserves-a-treat? I suggest the following:

—————————Power-everything; deluxe everything, including elegant, plush upholstery that doesn't look washable but is. (Remember: grandchildren!)

—————————A stereophonic sound system that refuses to play anything composed after 1960.

—————————A one-way ("don't call me; I'll call you") telephone;

— —————————A coded combination-lock door;

—————————An exterior secret compartment containing coded combination;

—————————Illuminated calendar-clock-compass with pull-out city map and address book;

—————————Auto jack and tire changing tools so complicated no one could possibly expect me to use them. (Such an enviable accessory would, of course, be extra.)

I didn't get such a car, but I did get my convertible. It was lemon yellow, with color-coordinated upholstery, power-everything; it was perfect, and I use the word "was" because it is past tense. In fact, it was never present. Before I could sign the contract and take delivery, my husband drove home one afternoon in a "surprise."

"Where did you get that?" I asked, as I surveyed the all-too-familiar station wagon.

"I knew you'd be surprised," he said. "The fellow at the body shop called me several days ago and told me they could fix our station wagon, and I told him to go ahead because I figured we could sell it. But when I took it over to Ernie's Used Car Lot, Ernie said it wasn't worth anything, so I guess we'll have to keep it. I'm sorry, because I know you were counting on getting that convertible, but we can't afford an extra car. I'm afraid we'll have to cancel the convertible. I'll call the dealer and tell him."

"Don't call before I get back," I said as I took the keys to the station wagon from him.

"Get back?" he asked. "Where are you going?"

"Where do you think?" I said, "I'm going out and look for a bigger tree!"

Notes From a Liberated Lady

I'm a liberated lady, I admit,
For I've written and I've lectured quite a bit.
But I still begin to panic
If a problem is mechanic,
And if I'm asked to fix an auto I will quit.

I'm a liberated lady, of a sort.
But when I compute my taxes, I abort.
Such calculations I surrender
To the masculine of gender,
So the IRS won't haul me off to court.

I'm a liberated lady, from now on;
But I'll never be caught mowing any lawn.
As for cleaning the garage,
I'm as good as a mirage;
So don't ever blink your eye, or I'll be gone.

I've been liberated lately, yes, indeed.
But I disfavor being freed with such speed!
I will leave to future sisters
Competition with the misters,
I am just about as equal as I need!

20 ✑

NOTES
FROM A LIBERATED LADY

Despite the fact that I long ago capitulated to the Women's Movement and allowed myself to be "liberated," I am having a hard time adjusting to all this equality. Oh, I rather liked the idea of coming down off my lonely pedestal and piddling around with a little career, and I *love* the idea of having my husband help with the dishes, but there are certain things that, liberated or not, I simply refuse to do. These include:

Look under the hood of my car. Refusing to look under the hood of my car may seem like stubbornness, but actually it is quite sensible. As long as I never look under there, I won't be expected to know what goes on in there. Of course I know what's *there;* there's a big black thing called a motor, and a little black thing called a battery, a bunch of cables and hoses, and a plastic thingumajig that's supposed to shoot water onto my windshield but seldom does. But I don't like to look at these things, because in the first place they are all dirty and greasy, and I get depressed that they aren't still as shiny and clean as they were when I bought the car; and in the second place, everytime I have peeked under the hood of my car something has either fallen apart, come unplugged, belched smoke, or spat at me.

I am sure my daughters are ashamed of me, as they are all cognizant of such things as distributor caps and spark plugs, oil filters and antifreeze, but frankly, it's all I can do to remember to keep the gas tank filled and the wheel tax paid. (Neither of which, evidently, my daughters know how to do.) I am not a mechanic, or even mechanically inclined, and if that makes me sexist, so be it.

I miss the days when a lady could drive into a service station and tell the mechanic: "My car goes 'ping-pong'; please fix it," and he would. He didn't ask questions; he certainly didn't expect any help; furthermore, he fixed that car on the spot, sometimes while the lady was sitting in it. Then, once the car was fixed, all the lady had to do was say: "Charge it to my husband," and drive off.

Nowadays, if a woman's car develops a "ping," she not only has to call and make an appointment with the mechanic (by which time the ping will either have disappeared or destroyed the transmission), but she also has to be able to describe to the mechanic, in detailed terms, exactly what is wrong with the car, as well as list the parts (including make, model, and serial number) that he will need to fix it. When she finally takes her car into the service garage (if indeed it is still drivable by that time), she will then be expected to poke her carefully coiffured head under that greasy hood, or worse, under that drippy hoist, and point out the problem areas to the mechanic, all of which may make her wonder why she just doesn't go one step further and fix the darn thing herself.

Fortunately, I have found a marvelous mechanic who is able to fix my car all by himself without my advice and assistance. He not only knows what a ping is, he knows the difference between a ping and a thrump. He refuses to listen to any attempted explanations as to how, why, or for what length of time the ping has been pinging or the thrump thrumping, and he never chastises me for such normal habits as riding the brake, failing to get a regular tune-up, or leaving my snow tires on all summer. He assumes that I am an absolute idiot about automobiles and acts accordingly, repairing and replacing where needed, and silently sending my husband the bill. Despite this chauvinistic attitude, I love the man dearly; however, I do have one complaint. It's almost impossible to get an appointment with him because, naturally, he's the most popular mechanic in town.

Fill out an income tax return. My parents accused me of marrying an attorney so I would have someone to fill out my income tax return. This is not true. It never occurred to me when I got married that I would ever be expected to fill out an income tax return because it never occurred to me that I would ever have an income. (I know it sounds incredible, but there was once a time when women who married got to quit their jobs and stay home, where they had *all* morning and *all* afternoon to do those chores many wives now squeeze into evenings and weekends.) For years, the only money I ever saw was the cash my husband allotted me for such frivolities as food, rent, and furnace repairs, and surprising though it may seem, the IRS did not tax housewives who accepted money from their husbands, though I have no doubt they will someday figure out a way to do so.

It was not until I started bringing in an "outside income" that the IRS acknowledged my existence and my husband concluded that if I was going to earn an income, I should know how to fill out an income tax return.

Since I rather enjoy a challenge, I agreed with him. After all, I am somewhat of an expert at filling out forms, having enrolled numerous children in kindergartens, grade schools, high schools, colleges, graduate schools, technical schools, and summer schools, not to mention the class I myself took in Assertiveness Training so I could figure out how to force my kids to fill out their own forms.

But no form I have ever seen can compare to the income tax form. Is it true that seventh and eighth graders master these things? No wonder they don't have time to learn long division or the conjugation of verbs; it must take them at least a year just to figure out page one of Form 1040A.

Though I must admit I never got beyond the first line of the form, because my husband launched the lesson with an explanation of percentages and tax brackets.

"Wait a minute," I said, when he tried to explain my tax bracket, "there is something I don't understand. If my income is so much lower than yours, why is my income taxed in a higher bracket?"

"Because we are filing a joint return," he explained patiently, "and your income goes on top of mine. This automatically puts you in a higher bracket."

"I have a suggestion to make," I said, just as patiently. "Why don't we put my income *underneath* yours, then I can be in a lower bracket!"

"That's not the way it works, Teresa," he said. "The wife's income always goes on top of the husband's income."

And who decided that? Somebody's husband, I'll bet. Well, if somebody's husband gets to make the rules, then somebody's husband can just fill out the forms.

There is no truth to the rumor that I refuse to fill out income tax returns because I can't figure them out. I could figure them out if I wanted to; I just don't want to.

Clean the garage. The same goes for cleaning the garage. I could clean out the garage if I wanted to; I could probably clean it even if I didn't want to. But I refuse to clean the garage because I firmly believe that it is not a woman's place to clean the garage. So what if her husband has learned how to bake a quiche, change a diaper, or do something even more traditionally "wifely": write a thank-you note to his own mother? That doesn't necessarily mean he should get out of cleaning the garage. God intended for *man* to clean the garage; it says so in the Bible. "Whereas, woman shall dust, and woman shall cook, and woman shall wash the clothes, woman *shall not clean out the garage;* so sayeth the Lord, sayeth She." (The Book of Betsy, Chapter IV, verse iii. New Translation.)

Frankly, I love my husband too much to upset the order of his garage. (Forgive me, sisters; some people are too old to change. Despite my determination to modernize, it's still *my* kitchen and *his* garage, even though he eats in one and I park in the other.) Like most men, my husband stores all sorts of "valuables" in the garage, and he expects them to be there when he wants them, or even if he doesn't want them. Years ago I did clean out the garage, and for weeks afterward he wailed: "I can't believe you threw out those perfectly good empty motor oil cans; you *knew* I was saving those!" and "Whatever possessed you to give away the old lawn mower? I know it was broken, but I could have fixed it!" That broken-down old push-mower had been rusting away in the garage for five years, and he couldn't have fixed it anymore than he could have fixed the grill on my car, which I dented every time I drove into the garage and bumped into that mower. He was lucky I didn't throw away the car.

Mow the lawn. Speaking of mowers, even though we now own a superdeluxe power mower, I refuse to use it. It's not that I don't know how to use it, or that I'm not strong enough to use it, or that I don't consider mowing the lawn woman's work; it's just that I don't consider mowing the lawn *my* work —anymore than I consider scrubbing the kitchen floor *his* work. Maybe that's a bad comparison. My husband has, on occasion, scrubbed the kitchen floor. Perhaps I should have said, "Just as answering the telephone isn't his work." To my knowledge, my husband has *never* answered the telephone. Although I will concede that mowing the lawn is no longer a strictly masculine job, I must admit that I still shudder whenever I see somebody's wife pushing a lawn mower around their yard. I can only hope that her husband is in the house pushing a mop around their kitchen, or better yet, taking all her telephone calls.

Changing tires, cleaning gutters, washing second-story windows: These are all simple tasks which I never used to do because I felt I was too weak, and which I never now do because I feel I am too old. Since my husband is the same age as I, he too claims age as an excuse, but there is no conflict on these chores, because five of our children are still living at home, and after all, what are children for? Although lately I have noticed that our daughters are sometimes almost rebellious about such things. Just the other day I asked Peggy to climb up on the front roof and scoop the dead leaves out of the gutters, and she snapped: "Are you kidding? You expect me to put my newly manicured hands into that filthy, grimy gook? Get one of the boys to do it; that's a man's job, anyway!"

Good heavens, I hope we're not going to have another Women's Liberation Movement! I'm not sure I can remember how to cook!

ABOUT THE AUTHOR

TERESA BLOOMINGDALE'S humor and wit have made her three previous books, *I Should Have Seen It Coming When the Rabbit Died, Up a Family Tree,* and *Murphy Must Have Been a Mother,* big successes and have won her many fans across the country. In addition to writing a weekly newspaper column, she has had articles published in such leading magazines as *Good Housekeeping* and *McCall's,* for which she was a contributing editor. Her other books, which were selected by the Doubleday Book Club and the Literary Guild, have been excerpted in dozens of newspapers and magazines in this country and abroad. When not at home in Omaha, Nebraska, with attorney-husband A. Lee Bloomingdale and however many of her ten grown and growing children are there on any given day, she can be found on the lecture circuit, where she is in popular demand.